Elmer Thiessen 2.50

See S. Corson " J. Whitton St
  Journal of Phil of Ed Vol 12, 1978
                          p 63 - 8

— See critique by I. Lloyd " The Rational
    Curriculum " — I have xerox - File L.

Towards a Compulsory Curriculum

Towards a Compulsory Curriculum

J. P. White

University of London Institute of Education

Routledge & Kegan Paul

London and Boston

First published in 1973
by Routledge & Kegan Paul Ltd
Broadway House, 68-74 Carter Lane,
London EC4V 5EL and
9 Park Street,
Boston, Mass. 02108, U.S.A.
Printed in Great Britain by
Northumberland Press Limited
Gateshead
© J. P. White 1973
ISBN 0 7100 7680 0

Library of Congress Catalog Card No. 73–82372

THE STUDENTS LIBRARY OF EDUCATION has been designed to meet the needs of students of Education at Colleges of Education and at University Institutes and Departments. It will also be valuable for practising teachers and educationists. The series takes full account of the latest developments in teacher-training and of new methods and approaches in education. Separate volumes will provide authoritative and up-to-date accounts of the topics within the major fields of sociology, philosophy and history of education, educational psychology, and method. Care has been taken that specialist topics are treated lucidly and usefully for the non-specialist reader. Altogether, the Students Library of Education will provide a comprehensive introduction and guide to anyone concerned with the study of education, and with educational theory and practice.

Nearly all contemporary writing about the content of the school curriculum conveniently manages to evade discussion of the most fundamental questions of value that lie behind proposals for change. New projects, syllabuses and patterns of curriculum organization proliferate, but most are based on purely pragmatic considerations operating within a broad public consensus as to what it is worth while to teach. True, there is an increasing body of more journalistic writing attacking current educational practices from a highly ideological point of view. But this is largely negative in character where the curriculum is concerned and it too offers little sustained argument about the central value judgments on which everything turns. Not that this is surprising. Questions as to what things are most worth pursuing in life or most worth teaching to others are notoriously amongst the most difficult philosophical problems and there is little agreement among philosophers as to how such questions can be settled. But the content of a school curriculum necessarily reflects a value position that is of no mean importance for the next generation. It therefore behoves those in education to be as responsible and rational as possible in the decisions they make.

John White's controversial essay tackles the general question of the content of the curriculum we ought to lay down as compulsory for all. He seeks to answer it in terms of principles derived from a fundamental ethical position which he vigorously champions and an analysis of kinds of human activities that seeks to establish important educational priorities. His concern for the freedom of the individual and his personal wants will no doubt find a sympathetic audience. The combination of this with a demand for universal education in certain basic disciplines is developed in an original and illuminating way. Discussions on 'worth-while activities' and 'forms of knowledge' relate Mr White's approach to other work in philosophy of education, and a final chapter vigorously attacks an array of fashionable educational myths which run counter to his thesis.

PAUL H. HIRST

Contents

CONTENTS

Acknowledgments

I owe a double debt of gratitude to both Professor Paul Hirst and Professor Richard Peters: first, for their pioneer writings in contemporary philosophy of education which first stimulated me to serious thought about the curriculum and have helped me more than any other work in the field, except, perhaps, that of Robert Dearden on autonomy as an educational objective, to shape the thesis presented below; and second for their detailed and constructive suggestions for improving the book's structure and argumentation. I should also like to thank Keith Thompson for some uncomfortably searching criticisms of my main argument in chapter 3, and John Hipkin, who was also kind enough to read and comment on the manuscript. Finally, I should like to thank my wife, Pat White, both in her role of colleague–critic and for giving me new heart on the many occasions when I decided not to go on. Needless to say, I would like to absolve all those who have helped me from all responsibility for the logical and other weaknesses the book may well contain.

I

Introduction

A British child born this year will not complete his education until he is at least sixteen years old. If, as is likely, the school leaving age is raised yet again by the late 1980s, he will not complete it until he is at least seventeen or even, possibly, eighteen. What kinds of achievement – in knowledge, skills, attitudes, understanding, and so on – do the educators through whose system he will pass expect of him by this age? What is the range of these achievements? Is he to have some understanding of economics, for instance? Or of comparative religion? Should he have learned to paint or write poetry? And what, roughly, is the minimum level of achievement expected of him in any item in this range?

These are not unreasonable questions. On the contrary; in any rational educational system they will be among the first to be considered. It is only when educationists know what any child is minimally expected to have learnt by the end of his schooling that they can plan activities, courses and syllabuses to lead him to this point. This applies as much to primary as to secondary education. What one is aiming at by sixteen or eighteen must help to determine what one teaches not only to the fourteen-, or twelve-year-old, but also to the eight-, or six-year-old. There is no break in this chain of rational planning. And it is only when these questions are answered that those responsible for teacher education can do *their* planning – can ensure that they are training enough teachers, in the right fields, and with the right qualifications, to meet these minimal final expectations. How else could they begin to plan?

In any rational educational system, therefore, it is of paramount importance to determine this basic minimum. It is a reflection on the British educational system that it does not attempt to do this. The law does not insist on any particular kinds of knowledge, attitudes or skills for every school-child, except for religious education, the only compulsory subject in all schools. This apart, the nation has no general expectations of its children. It is up to the head-masters – or the local authorities or boards of governors whose servants they are – to impose what basic minimum they will for the children under their care, or, if they want to, to impose no minimum at all. What any child learns at school depends on all kinds of contingencies: there is no regulatory mechanism built into the system to ensure that he leaves school having achieved at least such and such.

This book is an argument for just such a basic minimum, both for the *principle* that there should be a minimum and, more especially, for a certain kind of *content* in which that minimum should consist. It is, broadly speaking, a philosophical argument, looking at justifications for different curriculum activities and the fundamental assumptions on which they rest. These general principles are also related to more specific types of curriculum content which conform to them. Clearly there is much more work to be done in the detailed elaboration of this content: a philosophically-oriented argument of this sort can take one only so far. Equally, there may well be disagreement about some of the more theoretical structures in the book and about their more specific recommendations: it is notoriously difficult to reach objective agreement about the content and objectives of the curriculum and no doubt subjective preferences on my part have affected what I say. But I do not belong to that pessimistic school of thought which would consign all these issues to the domain of the purely subjective – as though what one thought children should learn were a matter of either personal taste or, as it were, the communal taste of the society in which one lives. I have no doubt that there is greater room for objectivity than is often supposed; this essay is an attempt to show just this. It is not intended as a take-it-or-leave-it blueprint for a reformed curriculum but as a discussion document, a document in a debate on the framework of a common school curriculum that is just beginning to gather momentum in Britain as the latest stage in the development of the comprehensive school.

Advocates of comprehensive schooling have not been conspicuous until recently in arguments for a common or basic minimum curriculum. This has been partly because the main priority has been to end selection at eleven plus, simply to *get children into* comprehensive schools. But it has also been due to the supposed 'English tradition' in curriculum matters, our reluctance to impose a uniform pattern of curriculum activities on all children, our libertarian insistence that as far as possible individual schools should teach what they think best and often that, within schools, children themselves should be given opportunities for specializing in activities of their own choice. But it is important to realize just how recent the origins of this 'English tradition' are. It is not wholly, but very largely, a product of the past forty years. The notion of a uniform basic minimum was well established here before 1900: the pioneers of state elementary education in 1870 and after insisted on 'standards' in the basic skills which all children were expected to attain. I need not mention the shortcomings of this system, since they are well known. But this early notion of a basic minimum has been given less than its due. After 1900 the notion vanished. Some would say that it was replaced, for the 95 per cent of elementary school children who failed to get to secondary schools, with the notion of a 'basic maximum', since the very success – such as it was – of the 1870 system was increasing the demand for non-manual jobs and this was held to be economically dangerous. Again, there is no need to go into detail here on the elevation of practical (i.e. manual) skills in elementary curricula after 1904. Whether or not this claim about a basic maximum can be substantiated, it is important to point out that there was a fairly strict centralized surveillance of the content of elementary education until the year 1926. It was only after that time that the individualism which is now so prominent a feature of our system was given free rein. As is well known, one consequence of this individualism has been the bewildering variety of curricular patterns at present found in our comprehensive schools. Possibly this is all to the good; and, if so, the whole argument of this book will be built on sand. But if it is, then this cannot just be assumed. We must not accept curricular diversity without thinking, or simply because it is part of our heritage (however recent this heritage). Neither is it enough to appeal to the rights of each school to decide its own curriculum: for it is precisely whether there is such a right that is at issue.

Before I proceed with the main argument there is one caveat. Some people to whom I have put my ideas about a common curriculum have reacted in horror. 'We don't want anything like the continental system of schooling in this country,' they have told me. 'We don't want every child in every third year class in the country studying the biology of amphibians on the second Tuesday afternoon of term, and so on. Inflexibility of this kind would be intolerable.' Well, I agree. It would. But I am not arguing here that all the detailed content should be identical, still less that it all be taught at the same time. The argument is, rather, that the objectives of the curricula should be the same for all children and, more specifically, that the broad content of the basic minimum achievements should also be identical.

In 1871 Thomas Huxley's committee on curriculum for schools under the new London School Board included in its recommendations for older children elementary social economy. This, it held,

3

should be an essential, not a discretionary subject. Do we think today, in 1973, that some understanding of economic affairs should be part of the equipment of every school leaver? It is perhaps not a question which comes easily to us. We now lack a tradition of claim and counter-claim against which to answer it. It is in the hope of helping to reconstruct such a tradition that I turn now to the substance of this essay.

2

Intrinsic values

Liberty and constraint

The first piece of conceptual apparatus we shall require is the concept of liberty. This is because talk of a minimum set of achievements expected of school leavers brings with it the notion of constraint – constraint on all pupils to reach these standards – and any constraint cuts across the liberty of the individual to do what he might otherwise have wanted. Any infringement of liberty is *prima facie* morally unjustifiable. If A prevents B from doing what he wants, A is satisfying his own desire (to constrain B) at the expense of B's. Since in this situation there are two wants to be satisfied, A's and B's, A has *prima facie* no good reason to favour his own. Any rational morality must insist on the principle of liberty since without it it fails in this way to be rational. But it is only *prima facie* wrong to prevent people from doing what they want, because there may often be considerations which override the application of this principle: it may well not be wrong to prevent a convicted sex-maniac, for instance, from following his desire to leave hospital. But any such overriding, as in this case, must be justified.

It is a feature of our present chaotic thinking about educational matters that this fundamental point about justification, which we are quick to apply to the encroachments of the tax man or the government planner, is not one which we readily apply to school curricula. Many children, who would rather be doing things of their own outside school, are constrained, as things are now, to sit in classes and learn French or maths, metalwork or grammar. Is any of this justified? We rarely ask ourselves. Many, it is true, do raise the question with respect to religious education, perhaps partly because this is the only compulsory subject on a national scale. But all sorts of other subjects are compulsory, too, at least as far as the individual child is concerned: what precisely is compulsory varies from school to school and from stream to stream within

5

schools. Perhaps it is partly because of this variety that there is not much public concern over whether this subject or that ought to be compulsory. But we should be concerned. Many children, for instance, spend years learning a foreign language. Perhaps all this is a waste of their time. Perhaps foreign languages are compulsory in some schools for quite irrelevant reasons such as tradition. What we need are some criteria to determine what should be compulsorily taught. To begin with, we need to examine more closely the kinds of consideration which justify an interference with liberty.

There are two such considerations. We hospitalize sex-maniacs because this is thought to be for the general good: if they were left free, other people might well be harmed. We take a knife away from a drunken man not only because he might harm others, but also because he might harm himself. Considerations of a person's own good as well as that of others may justify interference.

Applying this to education, it would be right to constrain a child to learn such and such only if (a) he is likely to be harmed if he does not do so, or (b) other people are likely to be harmed. Of these, consideration (b) is one basis of moral education. We are justified for this reason in teaching children not to cause suffering to others. Much more needs to be said about the content of the moral education required of any school leaver. I shall be saying something about this in chapter 4. But until that point I shall mainly be following through the implications of consideration (a): the harm likely to be done to the pupil himself if he fails to learn such and such. It is logical, in any case, to look at (a) before (b), since with (a) we shall be studying what it is for a person to be harmed, a notion which we must clearly understand before we go on to ask what it is for others to be harmed. To put the same point positively: a curriculum course is justified under (a) if it is good for the pupil. It is justified under (b) if it is good for others as well; but what it is for something to be good for other persons cannot be grasped until we have studied what it is for something to be good for a person in general, and this brings us back to (a). The content of moral education is not independent, therefore, of the content of non-moral education, i.e. of that part of a person's education directed towards his own good. To act well towards others, a man must know what kinds of things are good or bad for people in general, including himself. In this essay I shall be concentrating very largely on non-moral education as just defined; but this is a necessary preliminary to a more complete account of moral education.

One would be justified, therefore, in overriding children's liberty in their own interests. But to say this is not to say that one has any obligation to do so. It is not hard to imagine an educational system which constrained children to do things that were not in their own

Objects to promoting general interest at expense of individual

interests but in others'. Might this not be justifiable? Suppose, for instance, that it were in the general interest to produce so many technologists of different kinds, so many accountants, so many shop-assistants and so on: there would be nothing wrong, it might be argued, in using the educational system to train people for these different categories, even though any individual pupil had no option about which job he would do and might well find himself learning things which could not be shown to be in his interests. As long as the educational system were acting in the general interest, it need not also act in the individual pupil's interest.

But is this line of thought acceptable? If we are talking about a rational educational system, this must be one which can provide good reasons for its actions. If it acts in the general interest at the expense of the individual's, then it must be able to justify this. How? The onus is on the defender of the system: unless he can produce a good reason, we must conclude that a rational educational system must at least be acting in the interests of its pupils. The whole curriculum theory to be expounded rests on this assumption. It may be unfounded – in which case much of the ensuing argument falls to the ground. But the assumption is not arbitrary: given that an educational system could not be in no one's interest if it is to have any point at all, it must be in someone's interest. It could be in the interest of its pupils or in the interest of others or both. So far there is no reason to exclude any set of interests. Thus if it is argued that one should not forward the pupils' but some others' interests, those of the ratepayers, the employers, the community as a whole or whatever, some good reason must be available, if the educational system is a rational one, to support the one set of claims above the other. The argument is formally identical to the argument in favour of the principle of liberty given above (p. 5). Similarly, it, too, is acceptable only *prima facie*: it is defeasible by any good argument which shows that the individual pupil's good can rightly be neglected. That there may be such arguments applicable to certain circumstances I do not wish to deny. If one could show, for instance, that the human race could not survive unless X per cent of men had to be content with a form of life in which there was no room for intellectual or artistic concerns – a life which, let us say, it was not in most of their interests to have to follow, then one might well be on the road to showing that in this circumstance their education should be geared to the interest of the whole community rather than their own. There are clearly all sorts of further problems about this argument before it could be shown to be acceptable. But it is, in any case, applicable only to a certain contingency: it is not a general argument to show that in any circumstances individual pupils' interests ought to be overlooked. Since I know of no general counter-argument of this kind, I cannot usefully discuss what might defeat my defeasible claim in general.

Until some sound argument is produced to the contrary, I shall take it henceforward that any rational educational system must at least have the pupil's good in mind. But what is the pupil's good? It appears that the fundamental problem which now confronts us is no less than the traditional philosophical problem of the Good for Man. Until we know what is good for a person, we cannot know what is bad or harmful to him, and so we have no criteria for deciding when we are justified in restricting his liberty. In talking of what is good for a man we must distinguish between (i) extrinsic and (ii) intrinsic good. Going to the dentist is good for me, perhaps, but not intrinsically so. It is good as a means to something else, to my physical health, say. Why is it good for me to be physically healthy? Is this something good in itself, i.e. intrinsically good? Or is it good as a means to something which is intrinsically good – pursuing the life of reason, perhaps, or worshipping God? I do not mean to answer this substantive question at this point, but only to indicate the logical priority of intrinsic over extrinsic goods. What is good extrinsically is good ultimately as a means to something good in itself: the chain of extrinsic goods cannot go on for ever. Our first task must be, then, to determine what is intrinsically good. Our rational curriculum planning in the area of moral no less than 'non-moral' education must begin at this point.

What, then, is intrinsically good? Is the pursuit of moral virtue? Or mystical contemplation? The enjoyment of beauty and personal relationships, as Moore thought (1903, ch. 6)? Or the life of reason, as Plato thought? Or is it some combination of things like these? Each of these alternatives would give us some purchase on the curriculum. Suppose one thought, for instance, that the best form of life was one devoted to theoretical enquiry, aesthetic experience and, especially, love of one's neighbour – or, if you like, to the familiar trio, Truth, Beauty and Goodness, with Goodness at the apex of one's value-hierarchy and Truth and Beauty coming some little way below it. It is clear how one might begin to construct a compulsory curriculum leading to this goal. It would harm a child to be cut off from the arts and the sciences, for instance, since if he knew nothing of them he would not be in a position to lead the Good Life. We have the beginnings of a justification for constraining him to study these things.

A transcendental argument

Again, I am not interested here in assessing the substantive claim that the pursuit of Truth, Beauty and Goodness is what is most intrinsically worth while: this is only an example to indicate one way in which our justificatory problem may be solved. But there is another substantive claim in this area on which I do want to dwell for a moment, since it is of importance in contemporary educational theory. I refer to R. S. Peters's recent work on the concepts of education and 'worth-while activities' (Peters, 1966, chs 1, 5, 6). His central argument consists of two parts. First, an analysis of the concept of education, intended to show that education is, *inter alia*, an initiation into intrinsically worth-while activities, i.e. activities worth pursuing for their own sake. This is in chapter 1. Second, in chapter 5, we have an analysis of these activities: and here various theoretical and theoretical-aesthetic activities are claimed to be justifiable as intrinsically worth while in a way in which games or other simple pleasures are not.[1] This is why such things as physics and literature rightly appear on school curricula, not billiards or bingo.

Now without looking closely into the detail of Peters's argument, let me say a few words about the kind of difficulty which any such theory has to face. It is a point applicable not only to Peters's theory, which is geared to an educational problem, but also to those of other philosophers not writing about education but who, like Peters, have wanted to claim that some activities, usually cognitive or aesthetic ones, can be shown to be worth while, while others are not. I am thinking, here, for instance, of J. S. Mill (1863, ch. 2), of G. E. Moore (1903, ch. 6), and, most recently, of J. N. Findlay (1970, ch. 5).

The difficulty is: can such a theory avoid the charge of arbitrariness? Can it show that the elevation of, say, art and the pursuit of knowledge is universally valid, true for all men, or is it merely the reflection of a private preference? How, if at all, can one show that all men wishing to follow the most worth-while activities in life must be committed to things like poetry rather than things like pinball? Is this an area where 'musts' have any application? Goodness, in this respect, may be less problematic than Truth or Beauty. Perhaps here, we may feel, there are universally applicable arguments why all men must, *ceteris paribus*, keep their promises or not kill other men. Morality itself might be inconceivable or human society unworkable without such principles. But suppose I, say, respect these basic moral principles: is there any compelling reason why I should value art or science rather than spend my days in a snooker parlour or by the side of a trout stream? Two famous arguments, those of Mill and Moore, are now generally recognized to be insufficient. Mill argues that pleasures of the intellect are of higher worth than those of the body since those who have experienced both sorts come down in favour of the former. This is clearly not an argument which will give us the 'must' we are looking for. That those who have experienced both prefer the intellectual may or may not be true. If it is, though, what follows? It may be the case that everyone who had (in the past) experienced both, has rated intellectual pleasures more highly; but this does not show at all that everyone who in the future experiences both must come to the same judgment. It is always possible that those who have judged this way in the past have had the same subjective preferences.

Moore's position is equally unsatisfactory. It claims that we know by intuition that the pursuit of beauty and (in his case) of personal affection are the highest goods. But what if others come out with different intuitions? Suppose it is intuitively obvious to me that mystical contemplation is the *summum bonum* and that personal affection is way down the scale: how could one support Moore's intuitions against mine or vice versa? How far is Moore once again merely propping up his own preferences? Has he shown that these preferences are universally valid?

Difficulties in intuitionism have led more recent thinkers, like Findlay and Peters, into a Kantian or 'transcendental' type of solution to the problem. Now a 'transcendental' argument, if it works, will provide the 'must' we are looking for. A transcendental argument is derived from presuppositions. Suppose, for instance, someone casts doubt on the truth of the law of non-contradiction, that it can't be the case that a statement is true and not true. How do we know, he may say, whether or not the law is true? One way of answering him is to point out that one cannot deny it without falling into unintelligibility: what sense would it make to say that the same statement is both true and false? If one is using language to make intelligible assertions, one must be committed to the law. The sceptic himself was using language in this way, in asking his question. Since this presupposes the truth of the law, he must see, on reflection, that his question was otiose, that he must accept the law.

If we look more closely now at Peters's transcendental argument we see that it is of this kind. In place of the sceptic in the last example we are asked to imagine someone seriously asking the question, 'Why do this rather than that?' (e.g. 'Why pursue poetry rather than bingo?'). Peters's argument is to show that presupposed to asking this question is a commitment to certain 'higher' pursuits. The person who asks the question seriously must realize, on reflection, that it was otiose. By thinking about what is presupposed to asking such a question he will come to see that he must value certain pursuits, e.g. the pursuit of literature and science, rather than others. This is an argument applicable to anyone: it has the universality we have been looking for.

How does Peters establish his case? Ignoring the detailed and subtle introductory argument in the body of his fifth chapter, let me concentrate on what proves to be the crucial passage right at the end. In so far as a person asks the question, 'Why do this rather than that?', Peters claims (1966, p. 164)

> [the questioner] must already have a serious concern for truth built into his consciousness. For how can a serious practical question be asked unless a man also wants to acquaint himself as well as he can of the situation out of which the question arises and of the facts of various kinds which provide the framework of possible answers? The various theoretical enquiries are explorations of these different facets of his experience. To ask the question 'Why do this rather than that?' seriously is therefore, however embryonically, to be committed to those enquiries which are defined by their serious concern with these aspects of reality which give context to the question which he is asking.

This is the argument. It is intended to show that a commitment of a sort to theoretical activities – or at least to those theoretical activities like natural science, history and philosophy concerned with the nature of the world and man's place in it – is presupposed to a serious asking of the question, 'Why do this rather than that?' Peters makes it clear that his argument does not justify all the aesthetic activities, especially music: 'It might reasonably be argued that literature and poetry, for instance, are developments of a dimension of awareness of the world, while other arts, like music, may be creating, as it were, another world to be aware of. The latter would therefore, be more like games than science or history' (Peters, 1966, p. 163, n. 1). But if the general argument is valid, we shall at least have an argument which puts those disciplines concerned with the pursuit of truth in a privileged position and perhaps literature as well. But is it valid?

In one sense one could not but agree that a person who seriously asks this question is necessarily committed to the pursuit of truth. If he asks the question seriously, he must want a true answer to his question. But this is commitment to truth in a far weaker sense than that required by the argument. For to say that he must want a true answer to his question is not to say that he must be committed to the pursuit of truth in science (or history or maths or philosophy). He could, indeed, be a sceptic asking, 'Why should I pursue science, etc? Why not bingo?' If he is, he is certainly not committed to the pursuit of such subjects as science or history.

But there is perhaps more to the argument than this. The questioner must, to ask his question, 'want to acquaint himself as well as he can of the situation out of which the question arises' and this, we are told, will require some exploration of science, philosophy, literature and history. It must be stressed here that this cannot be taken to be an instrumental argument – that one should explore these things in order to throw light on the question. For this would make them at best extrinsically valuable activities, whereas the argument is designed to show that they are intrinsically valuable. It is rather that to ask this question presupposes some commitment to these activities, pursued as intrinsically valuable. But how far is commitment to them presupposed? One might well argue that some kind of understanding of them is presupposed. If a person is seriously asking himself which kinds of activities he should engage in, he must have some understanding of the different options. In so far as the options include the pursuit of science, philosophy, etc., he must have some understanding of these. This would not prove that he would have to be committed to their pursuit above other things, either in the weak sense of simply valuing these things for their own sake or in any stronger sense of 'commitment' – for two reasons. First, it has not been shown that understanding X implies commitment to X; and second, other activities – such as bingo or billiards, perhaps – as well as science, literature, and so on, might well also figure as options, and so far are on an equal footing with the latter.

The second of these points might be countered by arguing that science, literature, etc., are not presupposed merely as possible options, but in another way too, which is not applicable to bingo and billiards. The man who seriously asks himself what he is going to do with his life must have some idea of what kind of thing a human life is. He must have some idea of the boundaries within which he can choose. Someone, for instance, who was totally unaware of the hypothesis that men have descended from lower animals, or that human life has no divine purpose, would not be as well placed as possible to ask himself this question. One might argue therefore that at least some knowledge of biology – I am not sure how applicable the argument is to science in general – illuminates the situation in which he has to choose. It is not difficult to see how some understanding of philosophy and parts of literature might be equally illuminating.

This answer to the second of the two points seems very much in line with Peters's main argument. It enshrines what seems to me an educationally important truth, and one which is closely in tune with an argument I shall be developing in chapter 3 below. But the first point still needs to be answered: it is not enough to show that understanding of these activities is presupposed, one has also to show that there is commitment to (favourable evaluation of) them. On the face of it, it looks as if one could ask, 'What ought I to choose?', understanding something of the 'illuminating' activities, but still, when it comes to the choice, valuing something entirely different. Since Peters's argument is designed to show that science, etc., are intrinsically valuable, i.e. of such a sort that any rational man must value things of this sort for their own sake, this possibility leaves the claim unproven.

One way out of the difficulty would be to try to show that, despite appearances, understanding these activities did entail commitment to them. Peters does in fact discuss such an argument, not in the course of his transcendental argument, but somewhat earlier in the same chapter. (I should add that he no longer finds this argument convincing.) He writes (p. 147):

> In the case of such activities [as science etc.], a strong case can be made for Socrates' view that if a man does not pursue or at least feel drawn towards what is good then he does not really understand it; for the activities in question all have some general point which must be sensed by their participants and they all have standards of correctness and style built into them which give rise to characteristic appraisals. For a man to grasp what these activities are he must be on the inside of them and be sensitive to these aspects of them. Could a man really understand science, for instance, who was unmoved by the passion for truth and the concern about evidence and clarity? What sort of mathematician would a man be who cared nothing for neatness or elegance of proof? ... That is why we could and always would say of a man who seemed to refute Mill's hypothesis that he could not have understood what the activity was about. For to understand an activity is to be committed in some way to its pursuit.

There is a sense in which this conclusion is right, that understanding an activity like science does involve commitment to it. We may grant that a man could not understand science, say, if he was 'unmoved by the passion for truth and the concern about evidence and clarity'. In order to come to understand science, he must come to value these things. But this does not imply that having understood what science is, or, more generally, what other 'illuminating' activities are, one cannot give up their pursuit in favour of big-game hunting or anything else. This is not to say that it is false that understanding these activities brings with it commitment to them; but that if it is true, it is true only as a matter

13

of fact and not necessarily so. But the transcendental argument requires a necessary truth; if all we have is an empirical generalization, we are back with Mill: we cannot argue from the fact, if it is one, that all who understand both the so-called 'higher' and 'lower' pleasures opt for the 'higher', that one ought to choose the higher.

I should add that in his later writings (see 'The Justification of Education', in Peters, R. S. (ed.), *Oxford Readings in Philosophy: Philosophy of Education*, O.U.P., 1973) Peters makes more explicit an ambiguity which he sees in his original concept of 'worth while'. He points out that it could mean 'worth while' in the sense of an activity to which anyone could devote himself for what there is in the activity. It could, on the other hand, mean having 'worth' conceived of as a normative demand which the individual must accept, without the implication that he will find complying with such a demand particularly absorbing or satisfying. It is in Peters's view an unconditional duty connected with the ethics of belief. Peters wants to hold that the pursuit of truth is worth while in both these senses. But as he thinks that the more convincing arguments are for 'worth' in the second sense, and as he needs also the first sense of 'worth' to underpin the case for theoretical activities as activities, he sees a lacuna in his argument. For, in his view, a man might, on occasion, examine the grounds of his beliefs or the reasons for his actions in acknowledgment of the demands of truth. But he might do it rather grudgingly. Given the opportunity to do what he likes, he will always choose something less demanding like lying in the sun.

To return to the main argument: we must conclude, I think, that this 'transcendental' argument in favour of the sciences and literature will not do the job. This is not to say that other arguments will not be successful. But it underlines the fact, as I see it, that there is so far no valid argument as to why such activities must be rated by anyone as more intrinsically valuable than other things. Suppose a man with a knowledge of the arts and sciences decides to jettison any interest he had in them in favour of a life of idleness and comfort: can it be proved to him that he is somehow irrational, that rationality demands that in his own interests he takes the other course? For my part, I know of no valid argument for this. One may point out to the man that idleness may lead to such and such 'unfortunate' consequences – an inability to acquire the necessities of life, for instance. But one should not prejudge the issue: what may seem unfortunate consequences to us may not seem so to him. Poverty may mean nothing to him. He may even welcome it. Even the man who rejects the arts and sciences to devote himself to some 'utterly trivial' pursuit like combing his hair all day is not necessarily irrational. He may have a reason to prefer combing his hair – its pleasurableness; and a reason for disvaluing academic pursuits – their painfulness to him. No argument that I know can prove that he would do better to revise his judgment. None of this should be taken to imply that it is at all likely that anyone would jettison academic pursuits for such an alternative. Perhaps no one would do so. Perhaps it is a psychological fact about men that they tend not to prefer activities which are very simple and monotonous. But if so, it is only a psychological fact. Psychologically the prospect of a rational man devoting himself to combing and recombing his hair may be inconceivable; but it is not logically inconceivable.

Scepticism and the curriculum

Where does this leave us in the justification of the various arts and sciences as curriculum activities? If scepticism is in order, this means that it is doubtful whether they can be justified on the grounds that they must be, for anyone, intrinsically superior to other pursuits. In view of this, I suggest that we stop trying to justify them in this way and begin looking again at what constitutes the good for man in a totally different way. I shall come to this in a moment.

But before I do so, I want to look at some of the consequences, logical and other, of adopting the first position, i.e. of seeing the arts and sciences as pursuits which from anyone's point of view are more valuable than other things. This is a view which I suspect is pretty widespread in some educational circles, especially among grammar or public schoolmasters. One important objective of education on this view is to initiate children into the 'higher culture' of the arts and sciences, to commit them to these pursuits as an essential part of a civilized way of life.

A common objection to this approach is that it involves an unjustified imposition of the teachers' own values on their pupils. What right have teachers to 'initiate' children into this so-called 'higher culture', to 'commit' them to it? Just because schoolmasters tend to prefer this intellectual way of life, why should they impose their own preferences on others? Isn't this a kind of indoctrination rather than education?

I think there is a good deal of truth in this objection. I see no justification for trying to bring about such commitment if it has not been shown to be a 'must' for everybody. I would go so far as to say that it is morally wrong to do so: it is an unjustified interference with a pupil's liberty. Further, it also tends to pervert, I would hypothesize, a proper appreciation of the arts and sciences.

15

If one is taught to look on the pursuit of these things for their own sake as a 'must', one will tend to classify this, I suggest, under the same concept as other 'musts', 'musts' of a moral kind – telling the truth, being fair and so on. It may become difficult to separate these 'musts'. Cultural pursuits may well come to seem morally obligatory; one may feel morally guilty if one does not engage in them (compare the apologies which intellectuals sometimes feel constrained to make for having watched a programme on TV); efforts of will may come to seem as necessary to spurn the temptations of 'lower' pleasures for the sake of culture as they are in the moral sphere to combat one's selfish inclinations. All this is certainly true of my own experience as a pupil at school. Even in recent years I have been genuinely surprised at the sheer pleasure I have had from reading works by, e.g. Shakespeare, Pope or Tolstoy – works I have always felt I ought to read, and which, since I have always found moral obligations irksome to fulfil, I have left unread. *War and Peace*, far from being a burden – something I would have to sweat through for the good of my soul – proved an utter delight: its 1,500 pages could well have been twice as long.

There is this danger, then, in making children see culture as a 'must': what could have been presented under the aspect of delight or fascination is seen rather as obligation.

There is another danger. So far I have been talking about the child who, like myself, conforms to expectations, who comes to feel that he ought to be committed to the 'higher' culture. But there is also the child who does not conform, who rejects what his teachers say is good for him and turns away to, say, the pop culture, or other pursuits of his own. Is this desirable? Many teachers, these days, would be behind him. If it is morally wrong to try to commit children to the 'higher' learning, then isn't the child wholly justified in wanting to do what he wants to do, not what teachers think good for him? And shouldn't curricula be constructed far more around what children opt to do?

Reactions like this are understandable, but they are too extreme. It may be right to argue that children should not come to feel themselves committed to aesthetic and intellectual pursuits but it does not follow that they should not be introduced to them. It may indeed be true, paradoxically perhaps, that their education should consist very largely in just such an introduction. This is, in fact, precisely the position I would wish to argue, and which I shall later try to defend. But the method will be very different from any attempt to prove the intrinsic worth of these activities. The question, 'What kinds of activities are worth while in themselves?', is different from the question, 'What kinds of activities are educationally worth while?' If it cannot be shown that science and art are intrinsically valuable for everyone, it still remains possible that they are educationally so.

Values and wants

Curriculum-planning should not begin from substantive accounts of what the individual must value for its own sake, in the absence of valid arguments for these. It must begin in agnosticism and subjectivity. Moral considerations apart, we simply don't know, for a child on the threshold of education, of any kinds of activities or ways of life which must be intrinsically valuable for him later to pursue – or even of any which can be rated more intrinsically valuable than others.

But what sense can we attach to the expression 'the good for man' if we cannot give it any general substantive content in this way? Until we can answer this question, we cannot know what is good for pupils or what is harmful to them: so we cannot know what we ought to encourage them to learn or not to learn.

How can we answer it? Perhaps the best method is an oblique one. We do think we know in some cases what is good for people or harmful to them. If we examine what is presupposed in such beliefs, whether correct or incorrect, this may help us towards a clearer conception of the good for man. Let us take an example already used. We deprive a drunken man of a knife with which he has been playing in case he harms himself. Here we think we have a pretty clear idea of what would harm him, i.e. pain or physical damage. Suppose, however, we found out that the man had decided that he would commit suicide by stabbing himself while drunk. Would we then be so confident that wounding himself would be harmful to him? Our normal confident belief that physical damage harms a person rests on the assumption that such damage hinders him in satisfying his wants: if what he wants – as an end, not as a means – is to die, then being stabbed is not harmful to him. Preventing him from stabbing himself would not be said to be good for him since it would prevent him from getting what he wants (as an end). In this there seems to be an implication that what is extrinsically good for a person is a means towards achieving what he wants for its own sake. This in turn would seem to imply that what is intrinsically good for him is what he wants for its own sake. But this raises problems. A drunkard who was playing with a knife and not wanting to commit suicide might have wanted to play with it for its own sake, but this could scarcely be considered intrinsically worth while if, on sobering up, he was grateful to us for taking it away from him. If a person wants X for its own sake but X cannot be intrinsically worth while because on reflection he would not have wanted X, this leads one to a further hypothesis that what is intrinsically worth while is identifiable with what a person would on reflection want for its own sake.

obj' How acceptable is this hypothesis? A difficulty with the argument just presented is that it rests on what one might be inclined to say in a particular case. Here, as elsewhere, common usage might hide logical inadequacies. How far do reflections of a more general sort support this conclusion?

obj' There is, first, an assumption in this identification that the individual in question is in the best position to know what is intrinsically good in his case. Is this justified? Couldn't other people be in an equally good or better position? If the provisional subjective conclusion is right that there is nothing which can be said for all men to be intrinsically worth while, or more intrinsically worth while than other things, then it would follow that other people could not be in a better position than the individual. But it would not follow from this that the individual is in a better position than they are. This would still have to be shown. One cannot show this by arguing that what the individual wants for its own sake is intrinsically worth while and he is in the best position to know what he wants for its own sake, since the individual may always say *obj'* to himself, 'I know that I wanted to do X for its own sake, but was it a worth-while thing to do?' This would seem to argue against the identification of the two terms, since otherwise his question would be unintelligible: he would be saying, 'I know that I wanted to do X, but was it something I wanted to do for its own sake?' (I will call this argument 'A'.) A similar difficulty arises, however, if we move on to the further hypothesis, the one under review in fact, that the intrinsically good is to be identified with what an individual wants on reflection for its own sake. For here, too, argument 'A' is again applicable. That is, provided it makes sense to say, 'I know that on reflection I wanted to do X for its own sake, but was it a worth-while thing to do?', the new identification cannot be made on pain of unintelligibility. And if this is so, we have no reason to accept our original line of argument about the drunkard or, indeed, to think that the individual is in any better position than anyone else to know what is good for him. We seem committed to a radical scepticism: both he and others are on the same footing since they are all equally ignorant.

Answer But there are things to be said against this rather daunting conclusion. The main difficulty is that it now becomes quite mysterious what the sceptic might mean in making such a claim. His claim is that no one can know what is intrinsically valuable. In this he appears to be attaching sense to the words 'intrinsically valuable'. But what is this sense? If I can attach sense to the word 'red',

I must know what would count as something's being red or not-red; I must know the kinds of circumstances in which I would be justified in using the word. But what would be the sceptic's criterion for applying or withholding the expression 'intrinsically valuable'? He has not told us. Until he does so we can attach no sense to what he says.

A second point is that there may well be a fallacious bit of reasoning in the argument which led to the sceptical position. Just because argument 'A' was applicable to the identification of 'intrinsically valuable' with 'what is wanted for its own sake', it may not follow that it is equally applicable to its identification with 'what is wanted on reflection for its own sake'. (I will call these the 'first' and 'second' identifications, respectively.) For it may make sense to say, following the first identification, 'I want X for its own sake, but is it worth while?', since the questioner is comparing his present wants with what he might want having reflected about the matter. If this is so – and if it is not, the onus is on the doubter to say what else the question might mean – then while a question of this type can still be asked about the second identification, it does not lead to any paradoxical conclusions. For the question, 'I want X on reflection for its own sake, but is it intrinsically valuable?', may now indeed be an odd question to ask. One cannot take it as read, that is, that the question makes sense. If it is claimed that it does, the onus is on the claimant to show what sense it makes. This leads back to the difficulty expressed in the previous paragraph.

One possible line he might take would not get him very far, though it would show that the second identification needs to be supplemented in various ways. It is not at all difficult, he might say, to imagine someone asking himself the question at issue. A man who has thought over the things he has wanted for their own sake might well wonder whether what he now wants for its own sake is intrinsically valuable. 'After all,' he might say to himself, 'I've changed my valuations of my wants in the past, and I may well change my mind about my present wants.'

One may agree that this gives a sense to his question, but it does not get the sceptic very far, since intrinsic worth is still to be understood in terms of what is wanted on reflection. But the identification of the two must clearly be qualified, since what is wanted on reflection at time$_1$ may be different from what is wanted on further reflection at time$_2$. We need to establish some sort of criteria for what counts as 'on reflection wanting X for its own sake'. Would months of careful deliberation and exclusion of alternatives be sufficient? But suppose these were months of physiologically induced depression: a year later, in good mental and physical health, the priorities might be quite different. Again, suppose the careful deliberation had only been about a limited number of choices, a year later all sorts of other possibilities might reveal themselves and again the priorities might alter. This indicates, I think, that the want in question must be judged in terms of an ideal. In the ideal case what is wanted for its own sake on reflection is what a man would want for its own sake, given at least (a) that he knows of all the other things which he might have preferred at that time and (b) that he has carefully considered priorities among these different choices, bearing in mind not only his present situation but also whether he is likely to alter his priorities in the future. ((b) effectively rules out any preference adopted in a state of depression, euphoria, etc.: a depressed person is shut off by his depression from considering certain options which would otherwise be open to him.)

With this qualification, therefore, that what is wanted on reflection introduces an ideal situation, it has still not been shown that intrinsic value is not identifiable with what a person wants on reflection for its own sake. A further consideration may be introduced here to support this identification. Suppose there is a man who wants only one thing, X, for its own sake. He has reflected thereon, satisfying the demands of the ideal situation. Every choice but X he finds abhorrent. Would it still make sense to ask, 'True, he wants X on reflection for its own sake, but is X really intrinsically worth while?' The question implies that, granted something is of intrinsic value, this must be other than X. But everything else besides X he finds loathsome: perhaps, we might add, it makes him physically or mentally ill to engage in it. How could it be, we might ask, that anything of the kind could be intrinsically worth while for him? What would be meant by claiming this? Once again we reach the point, by a more dramatic route, where the onus is on the sceptic to say what he means.[2]

These are the reasons why I would favour the identification at issue. But there is still one more contentious point to be settled. This is whether it has been shown, after all, that the individual is in a better position than others to know what is intrinsically valuable for him. The qualification of the meaning of 'on reflection', with its introduction of the ideal situation from which to view one's wants, makes it doubtful whether the individual can ever know his intrinsic good since he can never as a matter of fact attain the ideal situation. Only God, one might say, is in a position to know this. As G. H. von Wright (1963, p. 110) points out, this may explain why some people despair of ever knowing their own good and in their anguish make this religious appeal.

But even though there are justified doubts about whether an

individual can know for certain what is his intrinsic good, it does not follow that he is in no better position than other people to know this. Knowing nothing of my wants, someone else has no grounds at all for saying that any particular thing that I may want to do is intrinsically valuable. But I am in a different position. Let us say that I have as broad as practically possible an acquaintance with the various things I might want and have reflected on priorities among these over a considerable period and come to a settled opinion about them. I have some grounds for saying that the ends I now prefer are the most intrinsically worth while since I am in something like the ideal situation – en route, even if I can never hope to arrive there.

One objection to the thesis of the last paragraph might be that in some cases other people could know what I really wanted better than I did: these wants might be unconscious, perhaps repressed: a psychiatrist might be aware of them even though I was not. This could no doubt occur, but a crucial point is that the psychiatrist could not be the final authority on what I really wanted. It is only when I avow that he is right that his claim becomes justified: it is my judgment on what I want that is authoritative (MacIntyre, 1958, ch. 4). A second weakness of this objection is that even though the psychiatrist (or someone else) could know what I wanted at any particular time even though I did not, it would need further argument to show that he could know better what I would want on reflection.

There are three noteworthy features of the intrinsically valuable as so defined. First, it is something formal, not substantive. We cannot identify it with any particular pursuit or way of life, the reflective life, for instance. (I would like to stress this particular example, since it might be held that the inclusion of the notion of reflection in the account of the intrinsically worth while shows that a person wondering what his intrinsic good may consist in must at least be committed to a reflective form of life. But this is not so. Just because the man has reflected on what he most wants for its own sake, it does not follow that the answer he comes up with must be some form of reflective pursuit. It might be: he might decide on philosophy or writing tragedies. But, equally, it might not be, since he might choose ten-pin bowling or swimming.) Second, it must be subjective in the sense that it can only be given substantive content once one knows what a particular individual wants in the ideal situation – and this may vary from person to person. On the other hand, taken at the formal level, it is the same for all men, and is in this sense objective. Third, as already remarked, it is something ideal, not in any value-sense of this term, but in the sense that, strictly speaking, it may well be unrealizable because of the conditions (a) and (b) stated above. Plato was thus right in seeing the Good as a possibly unattainable ideal, however much in other respects his conception of it differed from this one.

He was right, too, in seeing the need to plan the curriculum of the growing child so as to lead him in the end to an awareness of the Good. We do not know for any child on the threshold of education what the Good will consist in for him. This follows from its subjectivity. But we do know, in formal terms, what his Good will be. We know that only he can be in a position to determine this; and we know that he can determine this when he is in the 'ideal' situation, or, making allowances for the unrealizability of the ideal, when he is as close as possible to this ideal situation.

To do this, he must satisfy, as far as possible, conditions (a) and (b): that is, he must know of all the possible things he may want to choose for their own sake, and he must be ready to consider what to choose from the point of view not only of the present moment but of his life as a whole.

Educational guidelines

How far does this give us, as educators, any guidelines for action? Suppose we are impressed by the subjective aspect of the Good and adopt an extreme libertarian position *vis-à-vis* the child: not knowing what is in general good or bad for him, we do not know whether learning mathematics or French or what you will is good or bad for him and so make no effort to teach him anything, or at least anything he does not want to learn. This would be irrational. For letting children learn what they wanted in this way might well restrict the range of possible things which they might choose for their own sake: they might fail to learn about other things which might also have been included. Libertarianism of this sort makes it harder for a child to reach the 'ideal' situation.

Non-interference, therefore, may well harm the child, by restricting his options. The least harmful course we can follow is to equip him, as far as possible, for the ideal situation – to let him determine himself what the Good shall be for him. To do this, we must ensure (a) that he knows about as many activities or ways of life as possible which he may want to choose for their own sake, and (b) that he is able to reflect on priorities among them from the point of view not only of the present moment but as far as possible of his life as a whole. We are justified, therefore, in restricting his liberty as far as is necessary to ensure (a) and (b): we are right to make him unfree now so as to give him as much autonomy as possible later on.

I glimpse a possible objection at this point. 'Aren't you guilty of an inconsistency?', one may feel like asking. 'Earlier on you said that educators must beware of imposing their subjective preferences on children. But in all this emphasis on autonomy, on the need for everyone to choose his own way of life freely from as wide a selection of options as possible, aren't you holding up the autonomous life as an ideal? And isn't this just a subjective preference? After all, some people may not want autonomy: they may prefer to be slaves, or to let other people – or churches, or political parties – make their decisions for them. How then can the autonomous life be a "must" for everyone?'

Perhaps I should make it clear, in reply to this objection, that I am not advocating any necessary commitment to an autonomous way of life. The child 'must' become autonomous, to be sure, on the completion of his education: this follows from the preceding argument. But whether the pupil then choses to stay autonomous is up to him: if he becomes a slave or a 'true believer', that is none of the teacher's business, at least, on the argument so far: there is more, however, to say about this below (pp. 84-7). Autonomy, we might say, is a 'must' if we are looking at what is educationally worth while; what is worth while in itself as an ideal of life is quite another question.

But here another objection may spring out of the first. Granted that the argument has not claimed that it is necessarily good for the pupil to remain autonomous, it has at least claimed that he must become autonomous. It has claimed this on the grounds that ensuring this is most likely to be good for the child. But can this be guaranteed? Suppose on reaching something like the ideal situation, the pupil, after careful consideration of all options, wishes he had never been brought to this position, wishes in fact that he could have been left in ignorance. Surely, then, making him autonomous was doing him harm: the best thing to have done would have been to leave him alone.

But this objection is incoherent. Once he has reached the ideal situation, the agent can indeed opt for a non-autonomous life, as we saw in the answer to the former objection. But he cannot opt for having had a non-autonomous life. He may well wish this, but whereas one can wish that the past had been different, one cannot choose a different past. The pupil in the objection wishes he had been left ignorant. But it only follows that ignorance would have been good for him if he could choose above all else to have been ignorant, and this is logically impossible.

This alternative, subjectivist, conception of the good for man does leave us, therefore, with some guidelines which may help us to determine the 'basic minimum' for which we were looking in the first chapter. It enjoins us as educators (i) to enlarge as far as possible the child's knowledge of the different things he might sometime want for their own sake: there is no reason why the list should not include passivities (like being tickled) as well as activities, or vocational desires (e.g. wanting to be an engineer) as well as others; or desires to lead a certain kind of life (e.g. the ascetic life) as well as smaller-scale desires (e.g. to play the flute); and (ii) to encourage the child not only to learn about these different wants but also to reflect on them not only from the point of view of the present moment but also in order to establish some kind of long-term priorities of his own among them.

In the next chapter I shall look at the curricular implications of (i); and in chapter 4, of (ii).

3

Activities and ways of life

Let us accept, then, that as part of our 'basic minimum', we must
ensure as far as possible that all children know about the whole
range of things they might want to choose for their own sake.
It is important to stress that this is a desideratum not only for
'non-moral' education but also for moral education. For as part
of their moral education children must learn to avoid harming others
and to take others' interests into account in their own actions. They
must therefore know what others' good is – which may vary, of
course, from individual to individual. Now suppose a pupil does
not know about anything like the whole range of possible options:
suppose, in particular, he knows nothing about aesthetic activities.
Not only are his own options narrowed: his capacity for moral
action is also restricted. If he has to vote, for instance, on whether
the state should subsidize an opera house, he cannot fully enter
into the point of view of the opera-lover.

How far does this desideratum throw light on the question: what
kind of curriculum should children follow in schools and what
should its end-points be? I shall consider the topic under two heads:
(a) knowledge of particular types of activity (e.g. to go swimming,
to be a taxi-driver); (b) knowledge of ways of life (e.g. the Stoic
way of life).

Knowledge of activities: an important dichotomy

There is an immense number of such activities. Some come by
nature. One does not have to learn what they are (even though one
clearly has to learn what to call them). Examples are: wanting to
be fed, to move one's limbs, to play, to hold things, to lie in the
sun.[1] Since one does not have to learn these things, they are not
the educator's concern. On the argument presented in the last two

We do in one sense? 25

chapters, there is no reason why activities of this sort should not be, for some people, intrinsically worth while. This highlights the divorce I have been seeking to establish between the concepts of 'intrinsically worth-while' activity and 'educationally worth-while' activity.

Other activities cannot be understood without some sort of learning. These can be divided, exhaustively, into two classes, in which

(1) no understanding of what it is to want X is logically possible without engaging in X

(2) some understanding of what it is to want X is logically possible without engaging in X

This distinction is important, as I hope to show later, in determining the content of the curriculum. Here I shall try to determine which activities belong to which class.

That there are at least some activities that can be fitted into these two categories can be seen if we contrast (a) linguistic communication with (b) climbing mountains. (a) One cannot understand at all what it is to communicate unless one can communicate. For understanding what it is to communicate implies the possession of a conceptual scheme which only comes with speech.[2] (b) One can understand *something* of what it is to climb mountains without having climbed one. A person who has never set foot on a mountain can understand something of what is going on in, say, the film, *The Ascent of Everest*.

I pick these examples because they illustrate very vividly the contrast I have in mind. There is a further point which should be made about them. The term 'understanding' is troublesome. For the general thesis – that activities fall exhaustively into this dichotomy – to be testable, we need a criterion, or criteria, to distinguish 'no' understanding of what it is to want X' from 'some' understanding' of this. Now understanding any empirical concept has two aspects to it, the formal and the concrete. To understand, say, the concept 'red' implies, on the one hand, understanding something of the connections between this concept and other concepts with which it is logically connected (e.g. that red is a colour and, more generally, a property) and, on the other, the ability correctly to pick out instances falling under the concept (i.e. red things). Normally, the two aspects go together: one could not correctly pick out red things without understanding that red is a colour, and vice versa. Testing whether or not a person has grasped such a concept can follow either a formal or a concrete route. Most often, perhaps, it is the latter. We know that a child has acquired the concept table when he correctly distinguishes tables from other things. We do not require him to make explicit his implicit knowledge that tables are pieces of furniture of a certain type. Yet one can test understanding in this way: a man might show that he knows what mountaineering is by giving a correct verbal account of this. It should be pointed out, however, that a person can pass a test of either of these sorts only on the assumption that he would be able to pass a test of the other sort. If the child who could identify tables correctly could say nothing about tables in general, i.e. about what sorts of things they were, we might wonder whether his correct identifications were not accidents: and if the man who could define mountaineering could not pick out mountaineers, we might wonder whether his definition was acquired merely by rote. If we do not require a test of both sorts rather than only one, it is only because we are implicitly ruling out such possibilities.

The criteria I shall be using for 'some understanding of X' will be of these two types: either a correct verbal account, sufficient to distinguish X from other things, or correct identification of cases of X. It should now be clear that, on this basis, understanding what it is to communicate is rightly put in a different category from understanding what it is to climb mountains. A person incapable of speech lacks the concepts either to explain what communication is or to be able to pick out examples of people engaging in this activity; but someone who has never climbed mountains can both give some kind of correct description of mountaineering and point out examples of it.

With these preliminaries, let us now look again at the two categories and see more broadly which kinds of activities fall under them. The list of items is in neither case intended to be exhaustive. I explain why this is so below (p. 31).

(a) *Category I: No understanding of X is logically possible without engaging in X.* Some examples are as follows. First, *communication in general*, which I have discussed above. Second, *engaging in pure mathematics*. Neither of the criteria could be satisfied by someone who had not done any pure mathematics. He could not give a formal account since this would entail understanding something of the different branches of the discipline which, in turn, would entail some understanding of the conceptual schemes of each branch. But since mathematical concepts are *sui generis*, unanalysable into other than mathematical concepts, one cannot have such understanding without being inside the discipline. Further, since there is a hierarchical relation between these concepts, both within branches and between branches, it is impossible to give an account without having penetrated some way into this hierarchy.

If the formal criterion cannot be satisfied, neither can the concrete: to identify mathematical activity correctly requires the kind of understanding just described.

Third, *engaging in the (exact) physical sciences*. The same considerations apply as to mathematics: the concepts of the physical sciences – mass, force, etc. – are defined in terms of each other and are therefore unintelligible to one outside the discipline.

Fourth, *appreciating works of art*. This is different from doing mathematics or physical science in that one does not have to have penetrated into a hierarchy of tightly interdefined aesthetic concepts in order aesthetically to respond to works of art. It is more that the concept of such a response is itself *sui generis*. How could one begin to explain to a non-initiate what it was to look at a painting or listen to a piece of music from an aesthetic point of view? It would be no use hoping that one could define this in terms with which he was already familiar. The only way would be by letting him be exposed to works of art by a sensitive guide so that he will come to perceive aesthetic objects for himself. But, on reflection, even this may not be enough – if one is only exposed to one person's preferences. A further reason why art falls in this category is that the concept of art is itself what has been called an 'essentially contested concept', in that what counts as art is itself the subject of endless debate (Gallie, 1964, ch. 8). Is a work of art one which embodies 'significant form'? Or which expresses emotion? Or which reveals metaphysical truths? To study the arts is *inter alia* to become aware of the multiple and conflicting criteria of value which are essential features of these fields. It is not clear how someone who had never studied them could conceivably have this awareness.

Fifth, *philosophizing*. Philosophical thought, like aesthetic experience, requires a change of stance, a new way of looking at things. The 'things' in this case are not physical particulars, as in art, but concepts. Philosophy, unlike mathematics and physics, cannot properly be said to have its own conceptual schemes. There are technical concepts in philosophy, but they are not central to the activity since much excellent philosophy can be done without them. Philosophy cannot be explained to the layman because it requires seeing concepts which one already possesses – time, thought, pleasure, etc. – from a higher-order point of view; and to explain what a 'higher-order' point of view is, and which concepts are worth investigating, is to begin to do philosophy. Beyond this minimal characterization of the discipline, disputes tend to break out endlessly here as with art about the nature of philosophy as such: it, too, is an 'essentially contested' concept. Is the philosophical method linguistic analysis? Or is it phenomenology? Or rationalistic deduction from basic axioms? To understand what philosophy is is to understand how all these are included within it. This, again, is quite unintelligible except to a philosopher.

The peculiarity of category I activities is thus that no understanding of them is possible for those who have not come to engage in them. As stated above, the list is not exhaustive.

(b) *Category II: Some understanding of X is logically possible without engaging in X.* One can understand to some extent what it is to engage in activities in this category without engaging in them. This makes it equally possible to understand these activities as things one might want to do for their own sake.

Let us look first at certain activities often included in educational programmes: foreign languages, cookery, woodwork, cricket or other organized games, painting pictures or other creative aesthetic activities.

First, *speaking a foreign language*. Provided that one speaks one language, e.g. English, one can gain some understanding of what it is for other peoples to speak another, even though one cannot do so oneself. Many English people, for instance, who now fly to Spain on holiday are in this position. They can meet one of our criteria of understanding by being able to point out instances of non-English-speakers. One could also exhibit this understanding by satisfying the other, formal, criterion, i.e. by saying that foreign languages use different symbols to express the same (or in some cases different) concepts as our own language expresses, even though one had never learned to use these foreign symbols oneself. There is nothing inconceivable about this.

Second, *cricket* (or other *organized games*). Cricket, one might say, has its own concepts: 'over', 'run' and so on. But if one has never come across cricket before, one can learn these concepts without learning to play, for they can all be simply explained in terms of concepts which one already possesses, especially if one is able to cash these concepts by seeing cricketers at play. In this way one could come to give a formal account of the game sufficient to meet the first criterion. One could also satisfy the other criterion by correctly picking out examples of the game. (Thousands of television viewers could do this.) I should add that this understanding of organized games presupposes some understanding of what playing is, and it may well be the case that a person could not grasp what playing is without ever having played. But since play in general is a natural, not a learned activity, we may leave it to nature to provide this necessary experience for one's understanding of more determinate forms of play.

Third, *cookery*. Cookery also has its own concepts, but these, like cricket concepts, can easily be made intelligible to the onlooker who does not cook: and given that he has had some experience of eating he can see the point of the activity without difficulty. Again it would scarcely be too bold a step to take this nature-given experience for granted. Both criteria of understanding can clearly be met. This is also true for *sewing, carpentry*, etc.

Fourth, *painting pictures* (or writing poetry, or composing or performing music). This is an interesting case, because understanding these kinds of aesthetic activity is possible without learning to perform them, provided that one has understood something of the concept of art. One can understand something, for instance, of what it is to write poetry, even if one has never written any poetry oneself. But this understanding presupposes some experience of poetry (which might come through listening to it or reading it), for otherwise one would not know what poetry was. In this case, too, one can clearly meet both criteria of understanding without participation.

Several common curriculum activities fall, therefore, into category II. But so do a number of other activities. These include both what are normally thought of as 'vocational' activities and what are normally thought of as 'non-vocational'. (Admittedly, no hard and fast line between them is possible.) Vocational activities would include things like being an accountant or working on an assembly track. Both these, and virtually all other vocational activities, are intelligible without participation: one does not need to have worked as an accountant, for instance, to know what an accountant does. Non-vocational activities would include things like playing bridge or bingo, indeed virtually all leisure pursuits one could name. One may get some idea of these, too, without engaging in them.

If we take all these category II activities – the 'curricular' ones, the 'vocational' and 'non-vocational' together now – there is another important distinction to be made, cutting across them both. Understanding any of these activities presupposes a basic knowledge of one's mother tongue. This presupposes initiation into at least one category I activity, namely linguistic communication. But understanding some of these category II activities presupposes in addition to this some initiation into other category I activities, besides one's native language. As already mentioned, one cannot understand what it is to be a poet without some understanding of the arts; neither could one understand what it was to teach mathematics without some understanding of mathematics. Ignoring communication, other category I activities open the door to an understanding of all sorts of category II activities of the more sophisticated sort, both vocational and non-vocational. Less sophisticated category II activities do not depend on them in this way.

In order to understand what bingo or billiards, or working on an assembly track, or cookery or carpentry involve, one needs nothing more than some ability to use one's native tongue, given already that one has the relevant nature-given desires – to play, to eat, to move one's limbs, etc.

Four comments. This concludes the account of the two types of activity. There are four comments I wish to make by way of clarification or elaboration. Then I shall pass to two objections that are likely to be made.

(1) The activities mentioned under the two categories are not exhaustive. There are difficulties about producing an exhaustive list. The obvious one is that there are simply so many activities which one can pursue for their own sake. If one just takes games, for instance: there are many thousands of different games. And if one takes variants into account, or the new games (e.g. indoor games) that are constantly being invented, the class seems almost inexhaustible.

But this difficulty is not insuperable if one bears in mind the general thesis of this section, that the pupil has to come to know about all the different activities which he might pursue for their own sake. The question to ask is: will he be disadvantaged if he is not made aware of all the variants and sub-categories of different kinds of activities? I do not see that he would be. It is enough for him to know about the larger categories, provided that he also knows that there are sub-categories falling under these which he may go on to explore if he will. I do not think one can lay down any hard and fast rule as to what these larger categories should be, beyond saying that knowing what the larger category is like gives one a good idea of its sub-categories. I realize this is not very precise. Some examples will help. Soccer, rugby, cricket and golf could all be classified as 'ball-games'. But knowing only that these are games played with balls is not very helpful to our pupil-chooser since ball-games like these are so various. If the only ball-game he knew were golf, this might give him a misleading idea of the range of games in this class: he might think they were all like golf. He will also have to know something, then, about other kinds. On the other hand, if there are several varieties of the card-game 'patience', it may be enough for him to know that there is a type of card-game one plays by oneself: the varieties of patience may be more homogeneous than those of ball-games.[3]

(2) The second point is a particular application of the point just made to certain activities in category I. Take art appreciation, for instance. This is a category I activity since understanding its nature is impossible without engaging in it. But it may also be that parti-

cular kinds of art appreciation are also category I activities. It may be, for instance, that one could not understand what it was to appreciate music without actually doing so even though one had had experience of appreciating some other art form, like painting or sculpture. If so, music would be a category I activity. I am inclined to say that it is, as I cannot conceive of someone who has listened appreciatively to no music and yet understands what it is to do so. This is because such understanding is not conveyable by words. On the other hand, appreciating other art-forms may belong to category II. Appreciating sculpture may do so – I do not wish to be dogmatic. The test would be whether it is possible to understand what this is from a knowledge of other art forms alone. Other category I activities besides art appreciation may have sub-categories also falling under category I. Linguistic communication clearly does, in the shape of major categories already mentioned, philosophizing, for instance. Mathematics embraces subdisciples like algebra and geometry which may well also fall under the first category owing to their peculiar concepts. It is not the place here to go further into these relationships between category I activities, although I do take the point up again very briefly, on pp. 66-7. If the general curriculum theory I shall be putting forward is acceptable, however, these relationships will have to be examined in greater detail.

(3) The meaning I attach to 'engaging in an activity' needs clarification. This becomes evident if one tries to see into which category, I or II, an activity like playing chess would fit. One might argue that one cannot gain any understanding of it without engaging in it (and so it falls under I), since even the person who is simply given an account of the rules of the game and how they are to be applied must begin embryonically to go through the same kinds of thought-processes as an actual player: he must see, for instance, the importance of calculating the likely effects of making particular moves. In this respect, playing chess is unlike playing cricket: the distinction between participant and spectator is drawn in a different place.

This is a fair point. But I do not mean by 'engage in' anything quite as embryonic as this. Playing chess is a category II activity, since one can gain some understanding of it without acquiring the skills of chess-playing that only come through experience – the experience of pitting one's wits against another's.

(4) Finally, a further brief caveat, in case it is still needed, about what I mean by 'understanding the nature of an activity'. I am not talking here about a philosophical understanding. A person who has come to know, for instance, what artistic appreciation is is not necessarily able to give a philosophical account of the con-

cept of appreciation. He may not be able to state in words what appreciation is: it is enough for him to be able to discriminate between this kind of activity and others. This caveat has already been touched on earlier in this section, but it cannot be insisted upon too strongly, since, when I come in a moment to the educational application of this argument, I do not wish to be charged with over-intellectualizing the curriculum.

Two objections. I now turn to the two objections to the dichotomy between category I and category II.

(1) The first objection is that activities in both categories are not distinct, since none of these activities, including those in II, can be understood without learning to perform them. To take just one example. A cricket-devotee may argue that one cannot really understand what it is to play cricket until one has had plenty of experience at playing it: until then one can only grasp the externals, not the essence. 'But what of literature?' one might reply. 'Can't a skilful writer describe a cricket match in such a way that we can feel what it is like, as it were, from the inside – even without having played?' 'Even so', the cricketer may reply, 'this is very much knowledge at one remove. Real understanding must come from first hand experience.' Clearly this sort of discussion could go on much longer. But it is really beside the point. For what should be at issue is not whether one can gain a full understanding of cricket without playing it, but whether one can have some understanding of it, as measured by the two criteria laid down. That one can is surely indisputable.

(2) The second objection is the converse of the first: that activities in both categories, not merely category II, can be understood to some extent without learning to perform them. As Jane R. Martin (1970, pp. 85-6) writes:

> a myth has developed among educators that one cannot
> understand a particular discipline or art unless one has some
> competence in that discipline or art. There are any number
> of ways to understand any given thing and although it may be
> the case that an artist can understand art in a way that a
> non-artist cannot, it does not follow that a non-artist cannot
> understand art at all. Similarly with the disciplines....
> We need not worry that those disciplines which are not
> studied from the 'inside' cannot be understood.

But her argument does not prove her thesis. One may agree that a non-artist can understand art: one does not have to be a poet to understand poetry. But this does not show that one can understand

33

poetry without studying poetry; and the same goes, as I have tried to show, for mathematics, physics and the rest. That this is so is not an educators' myth: rather, it is, or should be – as I shall in a moment try to show – the foundation-stone of their profession.

But I have not, perhaps, done full justice to this second objection. What some of its supporters might argue would be this. The claim that certain activities like artistic appreciation and mathematical thinking cannot be understood at all without engaging in them postulates a 'preposterous discontinuity' between such activities and activities of a more unsophisticated sort. Science, for instance, is merely an elaborate sophistication of man's natural curiosity about the world in which he lives. Children at a certain age love collecting and classifying flowers, butterflies, birds, etc., and ask 'why?' questions of all sorts about them. Given activities such as these, they find no difficulty in understanding what botanists and ornithologists are about. The same could be said about artistic appreciation. The realm of the aesthetic is wider than the realm of art. A child with a good eye for natural beauty would already have some of the equipment necessary for appreciating landscape paintings. There are all kinds of degrees of understanding of the so-called 'category I' activities. Some understanding of a less sophisticated sort would certainly be possible without engaging in them.

This is an important counter-argument since it strikes at the heart of the case I am seeking to establish. But I don't think it quite succeeds. One can agree that there are links between category I and less sophisticated activities: art, science and mathematics have their roots in quite ordinary transactions with the world. But it does not follow from this that a child engaging in such transactions has any understanding of art, science and mathematics, or, at least – and this is perhaps the crucial point – any understanding according to the criteria laid down above (p. 27). A child of two may be able to use the words 'one', 'two' and 'three' correctly in application to groups of objects. Has she any understanding of the discipline of mathematics? In one sense, perhaps, she may be said to have this. She is in a different position from the child who has no number-concepts at all: she is, as it were, just across the outermost threshold of the discipline. But as I have been using the expression in this section, she clearly has no understanding of mathematics. She is unable to discriminate mathematics in any way from other forms of activity: this is still, no doubt, years ahead of her. Similarly, having some kind of aesthetic awareness is insufficient for understanding the nature of art. It is not enough to be crossing the threshold: one might, it is true, be immediately able to respond aesthetically to some of the simpler aesthetic properties of a landscape painting, but works of art are what they are because they contain within themselves the power to evoke more and more complex forms of aesthetic awareness. Works of art are inexhaustible in their ability to attract the contemplative eye or ear: new aesthetic properties constantly emerge with continued acquaintance. Until one has allowed oneself gradually to succumb in this way to the many-faceted power of art, one is in no position to claim any understanding of what art is. And it is worth a reminder here that the criteria for 'some understanding' are as stringent as they are because of their connection with the argument in chapter 2 about the intrinsically worth while: if the individual is in the best position to decide on this, he must know what different activities involve, so that he is in a position to choose or reject them as ends in themselves. A child who can use number-concepts or who enjoys hearing lullabies is not in a position to choose or reject mathematics or musical appreciation. The scientific example mentioned in the objection raises special problems. It is true that some sciences can be largely classificatory and still be called 'sciences'. A primitive botany would be in this position. A child interested in collecting plants might well have 'some understanding' of this science. But he would not thereby have any understanding of physics or chemistry. The exact (mathematical) sciences would still be closed to him as options – as, also, of course, would be the more sophisticated botany of today which goes beyond classification into realms heavily dependent on the exact sciences.

Curricular consequences of this dichotomy

The application of the dichotomy to curriculum problems should now be clear. Given that a pupil must come to understand all possible kinds of activities before his education is complete, he must be compelled to engage in those activities which are unintelligible without such engagement.[4] One comes back to the principle of liberty and justified overridings of it. If children were left free not to have to speak, study mathematics, physics, philosophy or contemplate works of art, then this might well harm them, since they might never come to know of whole areas of possible wants, both those connected with the pursuit of these activities for their own sake and those dependent on an understanding of these activities for their intelligibility. It might not only harm the child to be cut off from all these possible options: it might also, as we have seen, harm men in general if others were incapable of grasping what they wanted to do. The principle of liberty may be overridden, therefore, to prevent harm both to the pupils themselves and to men in general.

35

No such argument is possible, however, for candidate curriculum activities which belong in category II. Still keeping the premise that children must come to understand what it is to engage in cricket, cookery, creative writing, speaking foreign languages, gardening, etc., it does not follow that an educator is justified in compelling them to engage in these things, since it has not been shown that such understanding is impossible without engagement. There may be other ways of bringing about this understanding. The same is true of other category II activities, which do not usually find a place in a curriculum, like being a politician, a judge, a policeman or a deep-sea diver: it is important to ensure that children know what these activities are, but not necessary to get them to perform them.

The thesis in the last paragraph is important, if correct, since in many schools activities like games, cookery, woodwork, foreign languages and creative activities are compulsory. If there is no good reason for this, one can only conclude that millions of children are being quite unjustifiably compelled to spend their time on such pursuits. Conversely many of these children are not compelled to pursue all the activities falling into category I. This is equally unjustifiable. The Newsom Report, *Half Our Future* (chs 16-19), in its curricular recommendations is a remarkable document from this point of view. It almost goes out of its way to ensure that the 'less able' children with whom it is concerned learn nothing of the fundamental structures of mathematics and physics, while putting great emphasis on 'practical' activities, like handicraft and housecraft, falling under category II. Significantly, perhaps, it even recommends that these children learn French.

None of this establishes conclusively, of course, that category II activities have no place in a compulsory curriculum. Some or all of them may have. All that has been shown, so far, is that they cannot be justified in the same way as category I activities. There may be other proposed justifications. Each will have to be judged on its merits. One justification may be as follows:

That one can gain *some* understanding of cricket, etc. without engagement is not relevant. What has, rather, to be shown is that one can gain *sufficient* understanding in order to know whether or not this is something one wants to pursue, and to know what it is for others to want to pursue it. But sufficient understanding can only come through participation. Only experience of wood-carving can tell you whether or not wood-carving is really for you.

The first thing to be said about this kind of argument is that it cannot just be assumed to be sound (as it often seems to be). Since children's liberty is not to be overridden without good argument, the onus must be on those who put forward arguments of this sort to show that the sort of understanding possible without engagement is insufficient. The onus is not on the other side. Scheffler (1970, p. 29) introduces a principle of economy:

> Content should be selected that is judged most economical. Three types of economy are relevant. First, content should be economical of teaching effort and resources. Second, content should be economical of learners' effort. If a very strenuous way and a very easy way of learning something are otherwise equal, this rule would have us select the easier course ... Finally, we must consider economy of subject matter; content should have maximum generalizability or transfer value ...

In the present case we are especially concerned with the second of these. Children's time must not be wasted. In so far as the point of learning carpentry or rugby or French or singing is to extend the range of children's options, then there may well be quicker ways of doing this than by acquiring the relevant skills. I shall be returning to Scheffler's principle of economy in a more general context in chapter 5 (pp. 71-2): it is an idea which deserves to be stressed far more than it is in our educational practice.

A second point is that a good novelist or film-director does seem to be able to give us a more vivid perception, from the inside as it were, of what it would be like to engage in all sorts of activities in which we have not already engaged. I know now something of what it would be like to climb the north face of the Eiger – from a film, not from experience – and I am pretty sure that this would be one of the last things I would want to do. Is my evidence insufficient?

One should add here the very important point that imaginative devices like films and novels may well give one a much better understanding of category II activities than engaging in the activities themselves. The boy who learns about mountain climbing by climbing mountains is likely to be limited in his experience: his understanding of climbing may strictly be only of climbing, say, in the Lake District, or of climbing with such and such equipment, in such and such groups or with such and such skill. Books and films may well give him a more comprehensive picture of the sport than his own practice of it. Books and films are thus likely to be not only more economical in time for the purpose in mind: they are also likely to be more reliable.

It seems clear that one can have a very good idea of whether a category II activity is up one's street without participating in it.

One may still want to argue, however, that participation gives one more than a 'good idea': it clinches the matter. One may not know for certain that wood-carving is what one wants until one has done some carving. This may be true in some cases – though it is worth pointing out that even participation is no guarantee of a certain verdict, for or against: a man who has done some wood-carving may still not know for certain, given all sorts of competing options, that this is really for him. Equally, I am not altogether sure that one cannot sometimes be certain without participation, especially if it is a case of being certain that one does not want to engage in an activity. I would hold that I've more than a 'good idea' that I don't want to take up bull-fighting: if I'm certain of anything, I'm certain of that. Whether or not in general one needs participation to be certain may be a subjective matter, varying from individual to individual and from activity to activity. If this is so, then this provides, of course, a good reason for not insisting on participation.

But, in any case, why should certainty be required, rather than simply having a good idea whether or not one wants to do something? I see no reason why when it is claimed that a pupil must know whether or not he wants to pursue an activity this 'know' has to be interpreted as 'know for certain'. If he can have a 'good idea' about this which falls short of certainty, this, I would contend, would be enough. With one proviso: that the educational authorities should provide facilities for children to engage in all kinds of activities on a purely voluntary basis, so that those who still have doubts about wood-carving, for instance, can hope to resolve these through doing some, and those who are sure they want to do some can satisfy this want. (I say rather more about this voluntary side of education in chapter 5 below.) It is important that children are put in a position rationally to choose voluntary activities of this sort. With category II activities they can reach this position without participation; but a child could not rationally opt for a category I activity like art appreciation if this were among the voluntary options open to him unless he already had some experience of that for which he was opting.

A final point, bearing in mind the concrete educational issue of whether cricket, painting, etc. should be compulsory, is that children have very often had experience of something like these activities outside school. Children usually play all kinds of ball-games from an early age. They also sometimes help with the cooking or gardening, draw and dabble with paint at home. So even if, as I doubt, engaging is necessary for adequate understanding, it would still have to be shown that the kinds of experience just mentioned were insufficient. One would still have to show, in other words, why a curriculum based on such experience was necessary. This last point connects, too, with another issue which it is worth mentioning briefly. If one accepts my arguments about category II activities, one must still insist that school-leavers come to know about these, even though they do not have to engage in them. But this does not necessarily affect the curriculum, although it may do so. There would plainly be no point in building such knowledge into one's curriculum content if it is likely to be picked up outside. And, of course, by the age of sixteen or eighteen a pupil will have picked up an enormous amount of knowledge in this way. (With deprived pupils there is clearly a case for compensatory learning within the curriculum of what other children pick up outside.) For all or most children knowledge of many of the more sophisti-cated category II activities, especially professional ones, is possibly best not left to chance but built into the curriculum.

There are other likely arguments of a less general kind to sup-port the compulsory pursuit of particular category II activities: the arguments, for instance, that games are 'character building', that learning a foreign language makes one less insular, or that creative writing or painting is necessary for aesthetic appreciation.

There are many such arguments, and I cannot look at all of them here. None that I know, however, are persuasive, though this is not, of course, to close the issue. As regards compulsory foreign language learning, A. W. Hornsey, Head of the Modern Languages Department at the University of London Institute of Education, has written a stimulating paper called 'Why teach a foreign language?' (1969), in which he demolishes three common justifications:

(a) that languages are useful
(b) that we use our mother tongue better if we speak a foreign language and
(c) that the learning of a foreign language widens the pupil's horizons.

At the end of his paper his title-question is still open. Neither can compulsory languages be justified on the grounds that they intro-duce one to literature in the original which would otherwise be unavailable. By-passing the question whether translations of foreign literature are ever adequate, a central consideration is that litera-ture in general, without specification as native or foreign, can be made accessible to children through their mother tongue. Once one has acquired some understanding of the nature of poetry, drama, etc. through one's own language, one is in a good position to know whether or not one wants to extend this understanding outside one's native language.

Another justification commonly put forward for compulsory languages is that they are in the national interest since we need many foreign-speaking diplomats, salesmen, interpreters and so on. But this is no reason why everyone should be made to study a foreign language. Nor is it a reason why some (e.g. the 'linguistically gifted') should be made to do so. For the numbers necessary might be forthcoming if languages were voluntary: it would have to be shown that this was not so before it would be right to compel.

As for physical education, an interesting justification is found in R. Carlisle's paper, 'The concept of physical education' (1969). Deflating on the way the often heard claim (see the remarks below on Bantock, p. 95) that 'movement education' should find a place, perhaps replacing physical education, in the curriculum, he finally justifies P.E. on the grounds that its activities are best conceived of as aesthetic activities, so that physical education becomes a sub-class of aesthetic education. But a difficulty with this, indicated by Miss M. Adams (1969) in her reply, is that it is at most only an argument for watching games and gymnastics, not for participating in them.

It might, however, be argued that compulsory gymnastics and games are to be included in the curriculum because they help children to keep fit and physical fitness is a necessary precondition of being able to pursue any of the ways of life from which the child on my theory is equipped to choose. Now it is not clear exactly what 'physical fitness' means in this passage. The expression is elliptical: one is fit for something or the other. A person who is physically fit for working in a bank is not necessarily physically fit for boxing or running a mile. In so far as an aim of physical education is to produce specialized forms of fitness for athletic pursuits, this is no reason why it should be compulsory, for boxing and running, etc., are not category I activities. But in so far as physical education aims merely at promoting physical fitness for non-athletic pursuits, then it is not clear that the athletic pursuits it encourages are always necessary for this. This is more a medical than an educational aim, as James Mill (1825) pointed out in his article 'On education'. The school doctor, dentist and caterer are all concerned with producing physical fitness in children for non-athletic pursuits: so are the family doctor and dentist and the child's parents. No doubt further measures should be taken to see that children have good posture and so on. No doubt the school would be a convenient place where these could be taken (just as it is a convenient – but by no means necessary – place where other medical and nutritional measures are taken). But they are to be seen as an extension of the work done by the school doctor and cook, and not in the same category as curriculum activities.

As for creative aesthetic activities, these are often supported on the grounds that they are necessary for appreciation – that one cannot properly love poetry or paintings until one has oneself tried writing poetry or painting. I know of no evidence for this commonly held view, and I should have thought it easy to find empirical evidence against it, of poetry-lovers, for instance, who have never written a line. A weaker case would be not that creative activity is necessary for appreciation, but that it is helpful as motivation: it helps children to come to enjoy works of art, without being a *sine qua non*. This seems more plausible: it would rest, of course, on empirical evidence for its validation, and it would be interesting to see it systematically argued through. My only worry would be if this argument were used to justify spending more of a child's time on creative activities than was necessary to help him towards a love of art: I suspect that there is too much compulsory creative art work going on in our schools, especially in the visual arts and especially with the 'less able' child, which is not harnessed to this purpose. Other justifications are also commonly found: that children must 'express themselves' and creative activities help them to do this; or that creative activities are a necessary means of promoting mental health. I will not go further into these here, since they are discussed in R. F. Dearden (1968, ch. 7) and in my own 'Creativity and education' (1969). All this is not, of course, to argue that children should not paint or write verse or for that matter, sing, dance, play trumpets or throw pots. Let them do these things as much as they will. But let them do them voluntarily as and when they want. My doubt is only whether activities of this sort should be compulsory. Indeed, especially with the 'creative' rather than the 'performative' ones, there is something fundamentally odd in insisting that children engage in these. Is the experience of writing poems when it is the teacher, not oneself, who wants one to do so, likely to help one to understand what it is to write poems? Will it help to see this as the autonomous expression of one's thoughts and feelings?

These are, as already mentioned, only a few of many arguments in favour of compulsory curriculum activities in category II. There may well be others more substantial than these. All I can do here is underline that one must not simply accept any given rationale as valid: each one must be minutely examined. We simply have no right to make children learn things for inadequate reasons. Very often, reasons given are mere rationalizations. Sometimes the activities which they support have at their core a kind of curricular fossil, alive years ago at a different period of our educational history and now buried so deep in our curriculum-structure that it is apparently irremovable and given a totally different rationale from the one it once had, to justify its survival. Art is one example. The Cross Report of 1888 recommended that drawing be made a compulsory subject for boys in elementary schools as it promoted 'hand-and-eye' training. It was held to be 'the best kind of technical education at present available' and 'the foundation of all industrial pursuits'. The colourful dragons and spacemen who patrol the corridors of our junior schools are a far cry from the socially-useful sketches of the turn of the century, but they are also their linear descendants. Art teachers have changed their function. Or, at least, while their function in the old days was clear enough, it is less than clear today. New reasons are invented to help them maintain their positions. But whether, as I say, these reasons are more than rationalizations of an outworn tradition is open to question.

P.E., to return to this, is another example. Before 1900 this was not a compulsory subject, though a common one. But it would not be quite right to call it a 'subject'. As 'drill', it had a strictly utilitarian function, of helping to get children safely in and out of the new several-storey schools in which they studied. What was originally there for reasons of safety remained for other reasons. After 1900 detailed syllabuses were laid down for 'physical exercises', which now became compulsory. They were now a 'powerful factor in the formation and development of "character"'; they exercised an 'important influence in the development and specialization of brain cells' (Newton, 1919, p. 160). What previously had a perfectly respectable rationale was now being propped up by perfectly disrespectable ones. The contemporary malaise in the P.E. profession – its attempts to show that P.E. is every bit as intellectually sound as any other subject, its claims to be the Royal Society for the new Science of Movement or the Royal Academy for the new Art of Movement – all this unedifying nonsense can be seen in embryo in such 'reasons' as these.

This concludes the main part of my argument about the relation between the two categories and the compulsory curriculum. But before moving on to the next section, I must say something about a discipline often bracketed with those already admitted to the compulsory curriculum: history. How far should it be compulsory on the argument so far? It does not seem to me that history is justifiable in the same way as mathematics, physics and the arts, i.e. on the grounds that historical thinking is a category I activity. It does not require the mastery of inter-connected hierarchies of sui generis concepts like mathematics or physics: so far as I can see, there are no unique historical concepts. But neither can it be admitted on the same grounds as the arts, namely, that 'history', like 'art', is a sui generis concept in its own right, irreducible to concepts outside its own sphere. For what the historian does is essentially to tell a story about past events and their interconnections. Admittedly, it is not just a story, but one about the past which must conform to certain standards of objectivity. But, given that a child has been told stories from a very early age, he is already partly equipped to understand the nature of history. If we add to this the concepts of (i) past events and (ii) others' intentions, which he necessarily acquires in learning a first language, his equipment is even better. What is still lacking is an understanding that the historian sets up explanatory hypotheses which he then tests against the evidence available. But here I see no reason why someone with some understanding of physical science cannot grasp this side of the historian's work without having to engage in the activity himself. True, he may need to be told that the historian sets up hypotheses about unique events and is not trying to discover universal laws of nature; and also that he has to be extremely cautious, for such and such reasons, in his selection and interpretation of evidence: but none of this would seem to be unintelligible to the non-historian. If this account is right, then one would not be justified in compelling children to study history for the same reasons as mathematics or art. But there may be other reasons. A possible argument is that certain human wants are unintelligible without some historical knowledge. One could not, it might be said, understand what it is to be a trade unionist without some knowledge of the history and traditions of trade unionism. Or one could not understand the difference between a Catholic and a Protestant without some knowledge of the Reformation. The difficulty with this argument is that the minimal criteria of understanding emphasized in this section do seem to be satisfiable without knowing any history. A trade unionist ignorant of history might well be able to give an account of the aims and activities of his movement and to distinguish trade unionists from non-trade unionists; the same might well be true of a Catholic or a Protestant. Their understanding would indeed be incomplete and one-dimensional without the historical background, but on the criteria laid down so far this would be irrelevant.

As I hope to show in the next section, however, history does have a place in a compulsory curriculum; but it is justifiable in an entirely different way from that suggested so far.

Knowledge of ways of life

It is not enough to equip pupils with a broad understanding of wants which may figure as items in a way of life, for ways of life themselves may be among the things which men may want. One should also ensure, therefore, that pupils finish their education with an understanding of the many different ways of life which

43

they and others may pursue, that is, of the different kinds of guiding principles by which men may conduct their lives. I stress these guiding principles rather than more external features of a way of life. One does not understand the Eskimos' way of life by knowing that they live in igloos and fish through holes in the ice: one needs to know by what rules they are bound together in communities, how they themselves understand their own existence.

There is something unsatisfactory about laying down a list of the guiding principles embodied in ways of life. There will, on the one hand, be all sorts of intermediate cases; and on the other, it may be unusual to find any of these displayed in a pure form in any one person's life. Nevertheless, there do exist fairly well-marked differences between life-ideals, broadly conceived; and there is nothing to say that any particular individual should follow only one of them. I present the following list as a rough attempt to outline some of these differences. No doubt it could be refined and improved on:

1. A way of life devoted to the pursuit of truth, in science, history, etc.
2. A way of life devoted to artistic creativity.
3. A way of life devoted to others' good: the altruistic way of life.
4. A way of life devoted to physical prowess or adventure.
5. A way of life devoted to physical pleasures more broadly understood, including those of food, drink and sex.
6. A religious way of life, premised on the belief that this life is only a preparation for an after-life.
7. A life devoted to the acquisition of goods.
8. A life devoted to the acquisition of power over others.
9. A way of life devoted to reflection on how one should live.
10. A way of life devoted to domesticity.
11. A way of life devoted to public affairs.
12. The ascetic way of life.
13. A way of life based on a Thoreauesque return to nature.
14. A way of life based on one's surrendering to someone else the decision about what sort of life one should lead.

I would not hold a child's education as complete unless he became familiar with such different ways of life (this is not intended to be an exhaustive list). One may, of course, reject the pluralism in all this, i.e. the view that different individuals may have different ways of life and are none the worse for that. One may hold that there is a particular way of life which everyone should follow, thus translating a personal ideal into a moral imperative. This seems wholly arbitrary. Gulfs have existed since the beginning of civilization between one preferred way of life and another: no one has succeeded in producing a 'knock-down' argument that eliminates all rivals. Indeed, one may even be able to show *a priori* that there must be at least two logically indestructible ways of life: one presupposing that there is an after-life for which this life is a preparation, and one presupposing that there is no such after-life. If the existence or non-existence of an after-life is in principle undecidable, neither of these positions can be logically refuted.

Schools do, however, persist in moralizing preferred ways of life. In some the Christian way of life becomes moralized. In others (or maybe the same ones) it is altruism: readings about saints and heroes in assembly can all too easily incline some children to believe that they would be falling short, morally speaking, if they did not themselves choose such a life – yet the wholly altruistic way of life is only one of many. In other schools, again – and this is the most insidious of all – what begins as an unreflective prediction that a pupil will be leading such and such a way of life on leaving school becomes transformed into a moral demand: this is the sort of life he should be leading. Some teachers pigeonhole eleven-year-olds entering their secondary schools as future manual workers likely to be drawn into the familiar patterns of life associated with such occupations: in making their courses 'relevant' to the lives these children 'will lead', they do nothing to enlarge their vision of other possible ways of life, but merely help unwittingly to create in them the belief that the familiar working-class patterns are the ones they should follow.

Anything which can help to break the power over children of such imperatives is to be welcomed. Possibly one of the strongest imperatives in any society is that one should follow that way of life which others around one adopt; in a large-scale society like our own, the 'others' are not one's immediate neighbours but the impersonal masses who read the same papers and watch the same television programmes as ourselves: Heidegger's 'das Man'. It is all too easy for children to learn simply to follow the crowd, to come to think of their lives as running along immovable rails, and of the society in which they live as a massive, uncontrollable force to which they have no option but to subjugate themselves. This is where I think the study of history has an important role to play in freeing children from this natural preconception: by stressing the extent to which accidents on the one hand and the deliberate designs of men on the other have shaped events and by pointing out that our current institutions and practices are not timeless, that they did not exist before certain times in the past and may not exist in the future if men wish to change them, the autocracy of 'das Man' may be undermined. Children may well be able to gain

45

some understanding, as I argued in the last section, of different social institutions without a knowledge of their history. But such understanding alone may well merely reinforce one's belief that one is the prisoner of something timeless and unalterable: history can liberate.

History (including biography) has another role, too – not to reveal the contingency of the present, but to present us with examples of societies or individuals with distinctive ways of life: the Athenians, or the Aztecs, for instance, Socrates, Jesus or Leonardo. Other familiar curriculum-items can also play a part here. Religious studies would be one instance, though, in line with the general argument, much of the content that is commonly found in R.E. courses today could be omitted in favour of a concentration on more general, ultimately philosophical issues about the logical status of and evidence for transcendentalist claims about the existence of God, the immortality of the soul, the nature of worship and religious experience. Stress on detailed content rather than on more general issues may well lead children to become committed to the truth of the general propositions presupposed to more concrete religious discourse, thus making it more difficult for them to see the religious ideal as possibly only one among many.

Perhaps the most valuable instrument for extending one's acquaintance with different ways of life is literature, especially, though not exclusively, the novel and drama. There is perhaps no need to dilate on this, except to rue the very little part that reading literature for this purpose plays in most secondary school programmes, despite its immense educational potential. It has usually to find its place among all the other things subsumed under the general title of 'English': spelling, précis, grammar, creative writing, dramatics. And when literature's turn does come, instead of reading plenty of novels and plays to extend their awareness, pupils too often have to change into the slow gear of literary criticism and learn the skills of a new expertise, of which, since literary criticism is a category II activity, to revert to the dichotomy of the last section, they may gain some understanding in any case, without engaging in it. Some pupils, it is true, have the good fortune to read foreign literature in the original, although here too the stress is often on critical skills. The greatest pity – and this is, as far as I can see, almost entirely due to the historical accident that literature, for most children, came to be pigeonholed under 'English' – is that so few children leave school with any acquaintance with foreign literature in translation. (It would be interesting to know what percentage of school leavers have never read anything by, say, Tolstoy: and yet, from our present point of view, who better than Tolstoy to display before us so many and such deliberate contrasts between different ways of life that, as the author intended, we cannot help reflecting on them and evaluating them?)

We are growing used, in our present time of teacher shortage, to the development of new schemes allowing children to work very much on their own without having to pay constant attention to their teacher. A criticism of many of these schemes is that although children are actively occupied it is not always clear that they are learning anything. How strange it is that there is no comparable pressure to let children read more literature (and, we might add, since this is now a more general point, more histories and biographies)! Not only would their class teachers be relieved, but they would still be more obviously learners – to say nothing of the worth of what they are learning – than if they were fending for themselves on, say, a study of the 97 bus. Neither, indeed, would they be outside a 'teaching situation': they might well be sitting at the feet of supreme teachers.

Literature has, therefore, another role to play in a curriculum besides that of initiating children into the realm of aesthetic values as such. Philosophy, too, finds a place in this section as well as in the last, especially parts of ethics. It can help especially in the necessary task of assessing and comparing the different ways of life to which one is introduced. For it is not enough for pupils simply to know about these ways: they must still make up their minds which they themselves will follow. Philosophy can help by introducing them to arguments for and against particular ways of life or the presuppositions of such ways of life.

There is a problem here, as in the other topics just discussed, of knowing what would count as the minimal achievements in this whole area to be expected of any school leaver. Shall one lay down precisely with which philosophical positions he should be familiar, or precisely which novels, biographies and histories he should have read? This would be to lay too much stress on a particular content as distinct from something more general. Philosophy, literature and history are, from this point of view, only means to an end, and not the only possible means at that (certain films, for instance, may be included). All sorts of particular means are employable as long as the end is reached – and the end is that already stated: that a school leaver should (i) understand something of the wide range of possible ways of life open to him and to others and (ii) have begun to assess, to some extent, these different ways, so as to decide which he will follow. The difficulty comes, as usual, in stating what is adequate to meet this 'something' and this 'to some extent'. As regards (i), it should not be impossible to reach some kind of rough objective agreement about what kind of understanding would be required. It is clear at least what would

47

not be sufficient: the youth, for instance, whose imagination stretched no further than the life-ideals found in his local community, or who possessed no conception of living for a cause or idea, would not have reached the mark; while the girl who was able to make fine discriminations among types of religiosity or aestheticism would in these areas at least be far beyond it. Somewhere between these two our basic minimum in breadth and depth will have to be determined. (On the problem of basic minima in general, I shall have rather more to say in chapter 5.) As for (ii), since it concerns something that goes beyond the various types of understanding which are properly the topic of this chapter, it is perhaps best discussed separately in the following chapter.

Before we turn to this, however, there is one final point. I have been talking here about the way certain curriculum subjects can broaden the range of ways of life one might want to pursue for their own sake. But there is another, somewhat different, role to be performed here: not to exhibit actual ways of life, but to throw light on the nature of human life itself. The study of biology illustrates this well: biology as an empirical discipline does not reveal ideals of life in the way that, for instance, literature does. But one will have a grossly inadequate picture of man and his place in the universe if one has heard nothing of the theory of evolution. Other sciences, astronomy perhaps especially, but all to some extent – also illuminate this topic. So, too, do religious views – if we strip away for a moment their ethical recommendations, which belong more to the earlier discussion of life-ideals, and stick just to their metaphysical claims. Philosophy and the arts likewise have a stake in this area.

Many would argue that a main objective in education should be to encourage pupils' reflection on the nature of human life. The most valuable part of Peters's curriculum justification discussed in chapter 2 advocates this. I, too, am drawn towards a position of this sort. But why, after all, is this objective important? It cannot be insisted on as an intrinsically valuable pursuit for any man. It clearly has some extrinsic value as a prerequisite for choice of a life-ideal: one's life-ideals might change with a different understanding of man's place in the world. This would be enough on my theory to justify this as a compulsory curriculum objective. But there is something more. 'The proper study of mankind is man' not just to enable the individual to choose his own path through life. If it were, then if he has chosen his path, it would seem, he can henceforth drop any concern with the nature of man. Can he? To say so, one might argue, is to treat him solely as an autonomous agent and to ignore the moral demands which living in a human society must continue to make throughout one's life. As a moral agent one has, inescapably, to consider others' interests. But what one takes those interests to be will be shaped partly by one's views on the nature of man, by, for instance, one's belief about man's survival after death. Man is to some extent a mystery: and to that extent our dealings with others are equally mysterious.

This moral argument goes beyond the brief I set myself, to look at curriculum justifications from the point of view of the individual's interests alone. (I shall be saying more about the limitations of this point of view below in chapters 4 and 5.) Yet even this moral argument fails to touch the heart of the matter. True, one needs to maintain some interest as a moral agent in different interpretations of human nature. But the passionate concern, often the monomania, which scientists, philosophers, theologians, poets, metaphysicians of all sorts, have always displayed on this topic goes far beyond this. The final justification of its place in the curriculum must go back to the pluralistic conception of the Good Life: precisely because man's place in the universe has been (to some) of such perennial fascination, students must be encouraged to reflect on it since it may prove equally fascinating for them. Special provision must be made to try to ensure this reflection. This is because, although the topic draws on work in specific disciplines like biology, astronomy, other sciences, philosophy, theology and the arts, some of which already have a compulsory place in the curriculum, one can in principle study all these disciplines without bringing them to bear on the ungraspable fact of man's existence in the world. Reflection of this kind cannot be pigeonholed as either theoretical or aesthetic-contemplative. It transcends both categories. It is, likewise, forced on us when we begin to reflect deeply on the practical sides of our natures. Its transcendence of all other more limited concerns explains why some men in every age have found it of such paramount interest. No doubt some of our pupils will do too.

4

Integration and practical understanding

Suppose we limited this account of curriculum objectives to the recommendations of chapter 3: would they be adequate on their own? It is pretty clear that they would not. The pupil would so far have learnt something about all sorts of activities in which he might engage, and about different ways of life. But something would yet be lacking in his education, still seen as purely self-regarding. It is perhaps what many of those who press for 'whole-ness' or 'integration' in education have in mind. It is true that there is already an appeal to 'wholeness' of a sort in the stress on ways of life as distinct from discrete activities. If a child learnt only about the latter, he might emerge with a taste for boxing or painting or scientific research as isolated interests without having much idea of the various ways of life into which such interests could be woven. But, equally, it would not be enough simply to equip him with an understanding of different ways of life. For he could learn about these in a detached fashion, as objects of scientific investigation. They might then become just so many extra items which have to be assimilated along with his bits of mathematical or other knowledge. He could in principle fail to relate what he learned in both areas (activities and ways of life) to how he is to live his life. He must, therefore, come to see that his understanding of different activities is intended to widen his options, to give him the material for his choices, and that his insight into different ways of life is intended to give him patterns of organizing this material, patterns from which he may select his own way of life, or which, if he rejects them all, at least will make him aware of the need to adopt a way of life and help him to construct his own – is intended, in short, to acquaint him with the form with-out which the mere material makes no sense.

A further integrative task is therefore necessary, over and above the work on different ways of life. The focus is now not a way of life in general, but this boy's way of life or that girl's. This will no doubt vary according to the individual. It is at this point that the notions of a 'child-centred' education and an 'integrated' education meet: the child must be at the centre of all he learns; education cannot be 'subject-centred' in this sense.

This account of integration has affinities with R. S. Peters's plea for 'cognitive perspective' in the pupil, at least on one interpretation of this somewhat elusive phrase. Peters writes that a man could be highly trained in science but still lack cognitive perspective since he 'could have a very limited conception of what he is doing. He could work away at science without seeing its connection with anything else, its place in a coherent pattern of life. For him it is an activity which is cognitively adrift' (Peters, 1966, p. 31). There are two rather different ideas brought together in this concept, one, the idea of something's being connected with other things and, two, the idea of its having a place in a coherent pattern of life. The first of these ideas seems to be intended when Peters discusses 'cognitive perspective' again later in the same chapter. 'On the view here put forward an "educated" man could be trained in one sphere, e.g. science, and yet be sufficiently cognizant of other ways of looking at the world so that he can grasp the historical perspective, social significance or aesthetic merit of his work and much else besides' (1966, p. 44). Here the unifying principle is found in a particular activity, science in this case. Possessing cognitive perspective implies seeing the relations between this activity and other ways of seeing the world: science is the hub of the wheel, as it were, and the spokes radiate out from it. But if 'cognitive perspective' is interpreted in this way, it clearly falls short of the integrative ideal under discussion. For in this the hub is not a particular activity but the sense one makes of one's life as a whole. The spokes go out from this to meet the different elements – the activity of science, perhaps – out of which one constructs one's life. The scientist in Peters's example could be somewhat more than merely 'trained' but somewhat less than 'educated': not shuttered inside his discipline, since its windows are wide open on to other territories, but lacking any centre to his life other than this academic home. There is also a further problem about 'cognitive perspective' interpreted in this way. It is not necessarily educationally desirable that pupils should be encouraged to connect up different activities. Perhaps some activities just are self-contained. Music might be a good example. One could travel down spokes from music towards the physics of sound or towards mathematics; but the further one travelled down the spokes the more one would leave music as such behind. There is this danger, then, in over-emphasizing the links between different curriculum activities –

one which I mention in view of much current school practice – that the nature of an activity which a teacher is teaching becomes blurred and perverted: if a child is learning to love music, let him learn to love music as such, even though he never connects this up with history or science or geography.

The second interpretation of 'cognitive perspective' may, in any case, be closer to what Peters means by the expression. In this sense if a man is to be educated – or perhaps one should say 'properly educated' – he must see what he is doing as having its place in a coherent pattern of life. This is similar to the notion of integration which I have been stressing, similar to, but perhaps not identical with it. For when Peters argues that cognitive perspective is required in the 'educated man', he has in mind someone who continues to have this perspective once his formal education is complete. But the argument I have so far presented in this essay would not justify this requirement. From a purely self-regarding point of view, whether a person continues to think of his life as a whole on finishing schooling is up to him. It cannot be demanded of him that he do this. He may decide that the chaotic life is for him. He may prefer to live for the moment and positively value the excitement of letting circumstance shape his fortunes. Reflecting on how the elements of his life as a whole fit together is an educational ideal but not, necessarily, an ideal of life from the individual's point of view.

To return to the conceptual link I want to make between child-centredness and integration: it is important to take this claim at the right logical level. As I have expressed it, it is quite compatible with a curriculum based very largely on academic disciplines taught in independence of each other and obligatory for all children. This is not necessarily to advocate such a curriculum, but is merely intended to emphasize that the concept of an integrated, child-centred education does not contain within itself either the idea that disciplines should not be taught separately but merged into inter-disciplinary units or topics, or the idea that children should be left to choose what they want to learn according to their own interests. It is very easy to take these ideas of integration and child-centredness at too concrete or immediate a level. What are important educational objectives become transformed into class-room procedures, whose value is often open to doubt. Indeed, it is quite possible that in following these procedures one is actually making the objectives more difficult to attain. In the sense described at the top of page 51 that 'child-centredness' is at odds with 'sub-ject-centredness', it is equally at odds with 'topic-centredness': topics themselves are, after all, merely isolated items of a different sort and, unless carefully and comprehensively related so as to provide the child with the material for his autonomous choices, could become just so many totems to which the inner unity of the child's consciousness is sacrificed. Neither, second, will freedom of choice at classroom level necessarily lead to autonomy as an objective: as has often been pointed out, the freer the child is not to have to learn what is essential to autonomy, the less likely is he to become autonomous.

These conflations are two examples of a kind of misguided integrity often found among educators. If one believes in the autonomy of the child, so this line of thought runs, it is not enough to leave this merely as a slogan. Educational theory is full of such high-flown ideals: but they must be made to bite on educational practice. If one believes in the child's autonomy, one should, it is held, show this in one's teaching, here and now; it should be an all-pervasive feature of one's work. There are other examples. One may believe that the most important of educational objectives is the development of moral sensibility. There is much to be said in favour of this, as I shall be pointing out in a moment. But it is a misplaced integrity which seeks for this reason to lace one's classroom practice wherever possible with spoonfuls of 'moral education'. What is supremely important is not necessarily what is most urgent. Provided that the educational system is well enough organized to ensure that such ideals as autonomy and moral sensibility have their proper place at the apex of a school's endeavours, teachers need not try to introduce them into everything that they do. Paradoxically, the end may best be attained if for the most part it is ignored.

Let us return from this digression to a fuller positive account of integration in my sense, beyond the bare statement that the student must weave what he learns – rejecting some material, retaining other – into a total pattern of life. This will lead us later into a discussion of curricular implications.

There are two educationally relevant types of integration, one subservient to the other. The first is self-regarding integration: this is the construction of a way of life taking only one's own interests into consideration. So far in this essay I have concentrated for the most part on the self-regarding objectives of education. But an educational system would be less than rational if it saw to it only that the individual built up a way of life for himself based only on his interests. For if he did so, he would be open to that most devastating of objections to self-centredness: 'Given that the way of life you choose to adopt will affect others' interests as well as your own, why do you take only yours into consideration? What is so special about you as distinct from anyone else?' If his position is a rational one, he must be able to give good reasons for his self-preference: he must show that there are relevant differences between himself and others which justify this. Until such good reasons are produced, the individual cannot rationally deny to others that careful consideration of interests which he grants himself. And this is to say that what I shall call moral integration, i.e. the construction of a way of life based on a consideration of others' interests impartially with one's own, must take precedence over self-regarding.

The same argument may be extended to show also that some kinds of moral integration are more rational than others. To talk of 'considering others' interests impartially with one's own' is not to say anything of who these 'others' might be. One might conceive of a white South African, for instance, deciding to take others' interests into account in choosing a way of life and becoming a teacher or a doctor. He might even adopt a very altruistic form of morality, virtually identifying his own good with that of those whom he is serving. But the 'others' here may only be his fellow-members of the white community. He may fail to consider at all how his choice would affect the rest of the population: possibly it might even help in a small way to make their position worse. And here again he would be open to the charge of making distinctions based on irrelevant differences: what has a man's colour to do with whether or not one will take his interests into account? Moral integration is more rational the more universalistic it is, that is, the wider the group of relevant 'others'. In so far as we are discussing a rational educational system, its overriding objective must be to promote a moral integration in each individual of the most universalistic kind.

It looks as if we have now placed the keystone in the structure of argument that has gradually been built up and that there is nothing now but details to fill in. Beginning with understanding items of a very particular sort, isolable activities, we moved on to understanding whole ways of life and thence to the integration of both types of understanding in the construction of a way of life from a self-regarding and finally from a universalistic moral viewpoint. In this movement from particularity to wider and wider levels of generality under the supreme aegis of the (ultimately moral) good, the thesis has certain affinities with Plato's theory of education in the *Republic*, although I am not necessarily advocating this, as he does, as a temporal progression.

But though the main structure of the argument is now in place, in at least one way it is still rather radically incomplete. Something more important than a detail has still to be added. So far the discussion has only been about the ends which an individual follows: it is ends-in-themselves of different kinds – his own and others' –

Need for practical component — means to ends

that he has to bring together in a coherent pattern of life. But if this is all that his education has taught him to do, it will have left him rather disastrously in the air. He will have been superbly equipped for life in an ideal world – perhaps, indeed, the unseen ideal world of the *Republic* – where there are no obstacles of any kind – legal, financial, political, psychological – to achieving one's ends. For it is not enough to have got one's ends into some kind of order : to be more than a dreamer, one has to have some idea of how these ends may be attained, of the obstacles in their way, of how these obstacles may be overcome, and of which ends are impracticable since the obstacles in their way are insurmountable. We have been considering a form of education one of whose basic principles is that it serves the good of its pupils. But it will not do this, but rather be doing them harm, if it restricts itself to ends, ignoring means. Neither will the pupil's moral education – on which we have just touched in this section – be complete if he has a lively understanding of others' ends but none at all of how to reach them.

It is in line with the basic principles of this study, therefore, that the curriculum should contain a practical component. I do not mean by 'practical' what, for instance, the Newsom Report (1963, p. 128) means by 'practical' subjects. These, like handicraft or housecraft, are defined there as 'activities away from desks and classrooms, involving some form of physical skill'. Practical subjects or activities in my sense would be those which help one to understand means to ends, obstacles and ways round them. They will not necessarily require physical skill : some understanding of economic affairs, for instance, would seem an obvious candidate for this part of the curriculum.

I will look in more detail at the practical part of the curriculum in a moment. There is just one more girder meanwhile to fit into the main structure. This is an obvious point and parallels one I have made before. It is not enough for the curriculum to provide practical understanding of means to ends. The pupil could learn his economics, political science or whatever in a detached way, failing to link it to the logically prior consideration of ends. His practical understanding has to be connected in this way with his understanding of ends so as to meet the demands of self-regarding and moral integration. Neither type of integration is complete without this.

To turn now to curriculum applications. I have cast my net pretty wide in this chapter, having brought in not only the moral but also the practical side of education. Each of these would merit a volume on its own; and I am aware of a certain imbalance between the two longish chapters (2 and 3) that I have devoted to the curricular demands of intrinsic worth and the very few pages here on moral and practical issues. I will not here go into such detail on the moral and practical sides of the curriculum as I went into on the intrinsic side in chapter 3. This will be especially true of the moral side, mainly because I have concentrated throughout on the self-regarding justification of a compulsory curriculum. This has led me by degrees to the account of self-regarding integration. Strictly speaking, the self-regarding justification should have ended at this point. But it is just now that its limitations become most apparent. If the highest aim of education were to produce autonomous psychopaths it would be enough to end here. It was important to introduce moral integration to underline this inadequacy. But at this point we move over into the other justification, the other-regarding justification, which I first introduced on p. 6. The question prompting this is: what activities are we justified in compelling children to engage in having only others' interests in mind? I will not go further here into this many-sided issue. What I will do, in looking now at curricular applications, is restrict myself, first, to some brief comments on practical understanding and then to some even briefer comments on moral integration.

Practical understanding

To some extent we may draw on some of the arguments already worked out in chapter 3. For many, perhaps all, of the activities described there as activities pursued for their own sake could also be pursued as means to some other end. This is evidently true of things like linguistic communication, accountancy or carpentry, where extrinsic reasons are often at least as important as if not more important than intrinsic; but it is also, of course, no less true of reading poetry or engaging in pure mathematics. With regard to these activities, the conclusions of chapter 3 also apply here: it is important that the student knows something about them all, but only necessary that he pursues those in category I. The Newsom Report's 'practical subjects' – handicraft, housecraft and the rest – would not be compulsory subjects, therefore, in the 'practical' curriculum in the present sense of the term.

Many of these activities are extrinsically valuable as ways of earning money, i.e. as jobs. Practical understanding includes an understanding of different job-opportunities. The student will acquire much of this – especially as regards category I activities or those dependent on these – in the course of his curriculum studies. But this may well need to be supplemented by a careers information service to introduce students to the whole range of jobs they may choose and explain the different conditions of work. Careers information of this kind must be a necessary part of the 'basic minimum' for which we are looking. It is important to stress that on the educational theory I am articulating, this will properly be an integral part of a school's educational activity. It is not an appendage to the 'true work of the school', a somewhat sordid extra which allays the career anxieties of parents and pupils.

There are, of course, other things than the job one chooses which may facilitate or impede one's own or others' ends. Our student will have to know something about economic affairs – about industry, domestic and international trade, taxation and income distribution. He will have to know something about social, legal and political institutions; and about natural, geographical features relevant to socio-economic matters, resources of food and power, for instance. Perhaps Huxley's 'elementary social economy' of 1871 was designed to meet something like these requirements (see above, p. 3). At any rate there is clearly a need at this point to work out the contours of a basic minimum in this curriculum area other than the ones already described. It will perhaps be drawn partly from sociology, economics, economic geography and political science; and also partly from moral and social philosophy, so that, e.g. pupils are equipped to ask themselves under what circumstances in general it would be right to go against current law or custom. Whatever its content it must not leave the students with the idea that they must work within existing social institutions to attain their own and others' ends: it must allow them to see that existing institutions may and sometimes should be altered or removed.

There are also psychological as well as socio-economic factors which may affect one's ends. Students may face psychological impediments of different kinds, of some of which they may be unaware. Unjustified diffidence, anxieties about their sexual life, unconscious fears of different kinds, lack of perseverance, conformist prejudices – these are all sorts of blockages which may impede them. How far this points to courses in psychology, personal counselling, more novel-reading, sex education or just good teaching is not for me to say at this point. Once again, the main thing is to get the objective clearly in focus and see how it fits into the overall curriculum–rationale. Much of the work in this area, unlike others already mentioned, will have to be tailored to the specific mental impediments of particular pupils. But not all will be. Some knowledge of unconscious mental processes would seem to be a necessary condition of any pupil's self-understanding. And from a moral rather than a self-regarding point of view it is clearly important to be equipped with some understanding of the different kinds of psychological impediments affecting others' happiness. Much of this, I suspect, could be picked up from novels just as well as from a curriculum course in psychology. If such courses are run, they should at least be relevant to the general objectives we are considering. Too many university students of psychology choose this discipline because they want to know the inner workings of the human heart and find themselves disillusioned after a year or two, having lost their way somewhere in the middle of experiments on short-term memory or the physiology of emotional secretions or animal learning. It would not be progress if an elementary version of the academic psychology taught in universities came to occupy this very important place in the school's curriculum.

This has been a rather impressionistic account of the practical side of the curriculum and one not intended as exhaustive. Perhaps it will prompt more systematic analysis of this area. There is no doubting its importance. On the other hand, its importance must not be rated too highly. Teachers and educationists have sometimes laid undue stress on the intrinsically valuable nature of educational activities, sometimes even going so far as to make this definitional of them. A useful reaction has been to point up the value of practical activities, especially those of a socio-economic sort. But sometimes this reaction itself goes too far: the practical side of the curriculum becomes too dominant at the expense of the intrinsic. A particular and currently widespread example of this is the way in which so-called 'integrated humanities' programmes are organized in secondary schools. In these programmes, several traditional subjects, usually English, history, geography and R.E., are merged together. The 'integrated' content is very often a kind of social studies in which practical considerations loom large. Intrinsic values tend to get left behind. This is especially worrying as regards English. The subject called 'English' is a strange hybrid, embracing all sorts of things within it from basic skills to elementary linguistics, literary appreciation and creative writing. There may well be a case for its rationalization. But at least the English lesson has traditionally given children some of that insight both into aesthetic values and into different ways of life that I discussed in the last section. Not only this: it has often been the only lesson to do so. If English is swallowed up in a socially-oriented 'integrated humanities' there is a danger that these kinds of insight will be ignored.[1] Man is not to be identified with practical man: the sociologizing of the humanities curriculum undervalues the contemplative side of our nature.

I suspect that many contemporary British students of education associate philosophy of education with a conception of education as an end in itself and sociology of education with a conception of it as essentially practical. There may be some, perhaps less rather than more, justification for this in the recent history of each discipline. But there is nothing in the nature of either which need slant it in this or that direction. A rational education should give due weight both to intrinsic and to extrinsic values, for all the reasons I have mentioned. Philosophy of education and sociology of education each have important enough business to get on with: ideally, they work together in promoting rationality in education. It is not helpful to label them misleadingly as advocates of this or that educational prescription.

Moral integration

What curricular content can help in the task of reflecting on the manifold ends open to one and choosing a pattern of ends as a way of life, having regard not only to one's own but also to others' interests? To a large extent this will not be a matter of content at all, but rather of the manner in which different types of understanding are assimilated. As already pointed out, they must be acquired in such a way that the student comes in the end, if not always at the time, to see their relevance to his choice of a way of life. What one learns at school runs the danger of being inert in two importantly different ways. There is first, the danger of learning isolated facts within a discipline, facts which are not mobilized in judgments. But even when this kind of inertness is avoided, there is still the second danger of coming to acquire a new discipline but not reflecting on its value in helping one to construct a way of life. Subject teachers can clearly do something to avoid this second kind of inertness.

But certain types of content, too, may also help. Novels frequently revolve round this problem of constructing ways of life for oneself. Biographies and autobiographies are also obviously very relevant; so, too, are some philosophical works, especially in the ethical field. All of these could be fruitful bases for individual rumination or co-operative group discussion.

The student's practical understanding, too, must not be inert: he must have some experience in applying it to ends. This, too, is a *sine qua non* of moral integration. One could learn about economic matters as something interesting in themselves, and no doubt there is something to be said for this. But from the present point of view, this knowledge must be brought to bear on one's integrating task. In many cases the subject matter itself lends itself to this: the bearing of economics or political science is more obvious than that of, say, musical appreciation, so there is that much less danger of inertness in the second sense. Apart from this, I must leave it to those more qualified than myself to spell out the curricular requirements in this area in more detail.

With a school-leaving age fixed for so long at fifteen or below, work of all these kinds has scarcely been conceivable in the past for the great mass of young people. But as we are looking somewhat into the future and envisaging school leavers of eighteen or so, there is no reason why it should remain like this for long. It should soon become an urgent problem to work out the structure of this part of the school's job in much more detail.

But all these types of learning are still, in a sense, theoretical. Yet theory is valueless unless it subserves practice: judgment issuing in action is, after all, the real keystone. Educators must at least ensure that pupils do not leave school with yawning inconsistencies between their thoughts and their behaviour – wise and just in what they profess but rash or inconsiderate in what they practice. Again, this is merely a statement of an end rather than a discussion of how to achieve it. I will leave it to others to determine how these dispositions may best be developed.

5

Curriculum priorities and the voluntary principle

It is time to pull together the threads of the last few chapters. What overall pattern of a curriculum has emerged from the argument so far? How far are we now any clearer about what the basic minimum achievement expected of any school leaver might be?

While the previous argument has not sought to provide anything like a comprehensive blueprint for a curriculum, it has laid down some guidelines for further elaboration. First, school leavers must be equipped to understand enough about different ways in which they may want to spend their lives to enable them to choose their own version of the Good Life as they see it. This requires an understanding not only of kinds of activities, but also of kinds of ways of life. Each class should be as wide as possible.

Taking kinds of activities first, some of these must be pursued as part of one's education, since no understanding of them is possible without participation. These include speaking one's mother tongue, mathematics, physical science, art and philosophy. While many other activities must be known about, they do not need to be engaged in for this purpose and do not, on this argument at least, find a place in a curriculum. Educationally relevant examples are housecraft, handicraft, foreign languages, games and creative activities in the arts. Teachers should introduce children to activities in the former category not only as options which may be chosen for their own sake, but also in such a way as to open doors to understanding other activities which logically depend on them for their intelligibility. Mathematics and physics, for instance, open the door to an understanding of various types of engineering; the study of literature, to acting or creative writing; one's mother tongue, to innumerable things – from bingo and billiards, to foreign languages, housecraft and other practical activities.

School leavers must also know about as many different ways of life as possible so that their preferred activities may find a place within an overall pattern of life which they choose themselves. They should not be pressed towards any one particular way of life. The study of history is important here in making them aware that there is no natural necessity about the dominant ways of life which people follow in contemporary society. Literature also has a vital role to play in revealing different ways of life. This is over and above its role mentioned in the previous paragraph of helping the pupil towards an understanding of art in general. There is no reason why literature should be only English literature. Philosophy, too, has a place under this heading.

Literature, philosophy and biographical history are also helpful in achieving a second main desideratum in education, over and above a knowledge of different ways of life and ingredients within them: some ability to integrate this knowledge into an actual way of life. This integration must take into account both the individual's own good and others' good. Self-regarding integration must be subordinate to moral integration. Integration of both sorts presupposes practical kinds of understanding not already mentioned, like a knowledge of financial, economic, social and political institutions, and a knowledge of the impediments to mental health. This points to new compulsory areas of the curriculum: to an area of socio-economic studies on the one hand and an area of psychological studies on the other. In addition, a comprehensive careers information service is also a *sine qua non*.

The sciences versus the humanities

So much for the main features of the 'basic minimum', at least as regards its breadth. I shall be looking at its depth in a moment. But before doing so, I should like to say something about the relative importance of some of the different subject components of the compulsory curriculum outlined above. These may be divided, very roughly (there are obvious qualifications to make here) into three areas: the natural sciences (physics, mathematics), the humanities (literature and other arts, philosophy, history) and the social sciences. Now several contemporary curriculum theories do not include any hierarchy of curriculum activities: they insist on an initiation into a number of different 'realms of meaning' (Phenix, 1964) or 'forms of knowledge' (Hirst, 1965) – including, for instance, things like physical science, mathematics, the arts, philosophy, the human sciences, even moral knowledge – but are neutral about their relative importance. The theories themselves give no reason for thinking, for instance, that the sciences, natural and social, are any less important than the humanities. But, in fact, they are. Let us first compare the natural sciences with the humanities. This is to return to the 'two cultures' debate of some years ago. An important decision which one ought to make here is whether one is debating the intrinsic worth of these pursuits or their educational worth. On the first issue, following the argument of chapter 2, there do not seem any reasons, apart from subjective preferences, to rate the natural sciences any lower than the humanities. But educationally speaking they are in one way less important. Suppose we take two secondary-age pupils who, after a broad primary education, specialize for a few years, one in physics, chemistry and mathematics, the other in literature, history and, later, philosophy. Suppose, too, that they never study anything except their specialisms. The humanist would be inadequately educated. He could well have a good appreciation of the larger bearings of his life – of a variety of different ways of life open to him, of the moral considerations in these choices, of the need to integrate his life into a meaningful whole; he would also have some understanding of some particular activities he could pursue for intrinsic or extrinsic reasons; but he would lack an understanding of mathematics and physics and other activities dependent on these, and to this extent his options would be limited. But the scientist would not even be inadequately educated: he could scarcely be said to be educated at all. He would be a man without any general orientation to his life, apart from what he might pick up unreflectingly from his environment – at best, a specialist of genius but trapped within his discipline; at worst, a sophisticated serf.

The humanities have a more central role in the curriculum than the natural sciences, therefore, because they alone enable one to weave together a human life. As mere activities, they are on a par; but they alone are indispensable in the further, more integration-oriented requirements of chapters 3 and 4. They are also more important than the social sciences. A young specialist in this area would, again, not be inadequately educated but not educated at all. He might have a good knowledge of different institutions, of means to ends of different kinds – legal, financial, political, psychological – but he would have little understanding of ends themselves – not even how those connected with natural science – except in so far as his study of means itself became an end. He could well learn things about different ways of life, but only the actual ways of life of contemporary societies: he could not contemplate those unreal forms of life which a Shakespeare could construct from his imagination, or those real yet ideal forms which a Burckhardt (1860) could reconstruct from his sources.

The problem of depth

Let us turn back to the problem of the 'basic minimum'. We have looked at this in breadth. But in one way the hardest question still remains: what depth of achievement is necessary within each curriculum-area? How much initiation does a pupil require in the arts, say, or mathematics, before he has reached the basic minimum in these areas?

As I have just stated this, I have treated the question of 'depth' and the question of a 'basic minimum' as the same question. My reasons for this should be evident from the main argument so far. But not all would equate the two questions in this way. It is often said that an important objective, or perhaps even the objective, of education is the fullest possible development of the individual's potentialities. On this view the depth to which any pupil is initiated in any area depends partly on the pupil and his potentialities: one's aim as a teacher is simply to get each pupil as far as one can. As far as one can, that is, in the time at one's disposal: depth depends not only on the pupil but also on the age at which he finishes school. To put the same point in a different way, depth depends partly on psychological considerations – on the rate at which an individual can learn, for instance – and partly on practical ones – on how long the country can afford to keep children at school, for instance. Whether or not the breadth of understanding required of a pupil is universally determinable, i.e. as the same for all children at all times, this cannot be true of depth: this will vary from child to child and from decade to decade. No mention of 'basic minima' comes into this account.

As I see it, this psychological–pragmatic approach to depth is fundamentally mistaken. Let us look more closely for a moment at the concept of education which it contains: education as the fullest development of a pupil's potentialities. I do not know how many hundreds of times I have come across this description of education in examination papers of education students. I wonder how many, though, have reflected on the implications of what they write? I am not thinking here only of the value-neutrality of 'potentialities', of whether if a pupil has evil potentialities it is education's task to develop these as fully as possible. What is more puzzling is what this phrase, 'the fullest development of one's potentialities' is to be taken to mean. 'Potentialities' can be used in two importantly different senses. (i) It can be used in the sense of 'potential'. This implies limitation: it is logically impossible to outstrip one's potential, since one's potential is all one can achieve. If education aims at maximum development in this sense of 'potentiality', it satisfies this aim when pupils are brought to the uttermost limits of what they

64

can achieve. But one difficulty with this is that it assumes that children do have achievement-potential. But this is not something that can be taken for granted, as I discuss more fully below (p. 98). It is not at all clear, at least for normal children, that there are ceilings of general ability or of specialized ability in the different curriculum areas, beyond which they cannot go. One paradoxical consequence of the present view is that since it is only with certain mental defectives that we seem to have fairly strong grounds in postulating ceilings at all – e.g. the scantiest rudiments of speech – perhaps only those commonly called 'ineducable' are capable of being educated! (ii) The second sense of 'potentiality' does not imply limitation. If a person is born with the potentiality to speak, he is born with the power, as yet unrealized, to speak – and this says nothing about what he could never do. Is educating to be taken, now, as developing a pupil's powers as far as one can (say, in the time he is at school)? This is perhaps how the slogan under discussion is more commonly understood, but this too is not without difficulties. To bypass the problem of undesirable powers, on which I have already touched, let us assume that the 'powers' referred to are educationally relevant – the power to appreciate works of art, to think mathematically and so on. (It does not matter if one does not accept the particular educational theory I have been advocating: potentialities as a cook or musician or gymnast may equally be included.) Now suppose, as educators, we are confronted with a rather exceptional child who picks up the mathematics he is taught with ease and who gives every sign of being able to reach postgraduate levels of achievement in the area by the age of fourteen or fifteen. Is our duty to help him along the mathematical road as far as this point (or further)? On the theory we are considering, it would be. But what is the justification for this? Is there no limit on the extent to which such initiation should be compulsory? Suppose we make the situation more extreme. A pupil's age, we should remember, is only important for practical reasons, like the size of the education budget. Our duty as educators is to develop his potentialities as far as we can. If at twenty-five or thirty he is still capable of development, not at postgraduate levels in mathematics only but at equally sophisticated levels in all sorts of other fields, his education is still incomplete: if financial resources permitted this, we should ideally be helping him further down these different roads.

But there is something monstrous about this suggestion. The aim of compulsory education cannot be to promote the fullest possible developments of an individual's intellectual powers, for there seems to be no reason why anyone should be constrained to continue his studies in different areas to, say, postgraduate level. We must ask ourselves how far we are justified in initiating children into the different curriculum-areas. And the answer already given is that constraint must be kept to a minimum, a 'basic minimum' compatible with the pupil's learning all that he has to learn for his education to be complete. The issue of 'depth' cannot, in other words, be separated from that of a 'basic minimum'.

How, then, does one determine this basic minimum in detail? To look at a specific example: how much initiation does a pupil require in the arts before he has reached his basic minimum in this particular area? How far does the general argument in this essay help us to answer this?

It does give us some clue. He has to acquire enough understanding of art to enable him to know whether or not he wants to spend time (a) contemplating works of art or (b) engaging in logically higher-order aesthetic activities, like creation or performance. Some achievements would clearly fall short of this – having listened to only one piece of poetry, for instance, while knowing nothing of music or painting at all; others would be as obviously too far above the mark as this would be below it – being able, for instance, to write sensitive critical studies of works of art of many different styles and in many different media. The criterion we want of a basic aesthetic understanding clearly falls somewhere within this range. If we can agree on this much, this would seem to suggest that there is some hope for objective agreement when one turns to details. The pupil will have to be acquainted with many different types of works of art before he builds up, from their criss-crossing similarities and differences, an adequate understanding of what art is. Could any particular art form be left out of his education entirely? Could sculpture, say, be skipped if painting were included, along with literature and music? One test would be whether one could understand anything of the aesthetic interest of works of sculpture simply on the basis of one's acquaintance with other art forms, but without actually seeing any sculpture – perhaps simply from an oral description. Another test would be whether with such a background in the other arts one could pick out the aesthetically relevant features of any first piece of sculpture with which one was presented. Could one? I would be less doubtful about this than about whether one could understand what it was for music to be aesthetically interesting if one had never heard any but knew only about painting, sculpture and architecture. But it would have to be left to experts within the artistic area to work out more detailed priorities of this sort: experts, however, not in isolated specialisms, but men with some understanding of the different arts and what might be called their orders of intelligibility relationships as just exemplified.[1] This applies, too, to such relationships not only between the different major art forms, but also within any particular form itself. I see

66

no reason why experts on aesthetic education should not be able roughly to agree, provided their sympathies were liberal enough, on what criteria of understanding a student would have to meet in order to satisfy conditions (a) and (b) mentioned at the beginning of this paragraph. Rough agreement, within fairly tolerant boundaries, is all that one could reasonably expect here: one should not insist on anything very precise, since understanding is not an all-or-nothing phenomenon but develops by degrees. There is, however, one further guideline here which should help to narrow any area of disagreement. It follows from the insistence on the principles of liberty in this essay that the presumption is that the pupil should be obliged to study as little as possible. The experts should bear this in mind in laying down their minimal criteria of understanding and keep them as unsophisticated as is consonant with the purposes they have in view.

These points apply as much to theoretical disciplines as to the arts. In mathematics, for instance, an acquaintance with the four basic processes, fractions and decimals clearly falls below the minimum. This gives one neither an insight into the fascination of pure mathematics nor an understanding of the application of mathematics in some of the more sophisticated professions. But how far does one have to penetrate through the conceptual hierarchies of different branches of mathematics in order to achieve these? Once again, it is fairly clear what would be too good an achievement: a first degree in the subject, perhaps. But what, roughly speaking, the basic minimum would be is again a question for the experts.

What, though, of the knowledge of ways of life and the 'integration' described in chapters 3 and 4? It may seem odd to talk of basic minima here – odder than in mathematics, say, where we are used to examinations for school leavers, which attempt something of this kind. But I see no reason in principle why minima cannot be worked out in these other areas also. As for ways of life, I pointed out above (p. 48) that one could see what would show too little understanding – a lack of awareness of any ways of life except those approved in one's local community; and also what would be plainly more than sufficient – an ability to make fine discriminations between all sorts of life-styles. Somewhere between these two extremes will be the minimum understanding for which we are looking. It is true that there are no experts in ways of life as there are in mathematics, although philosophers, sociologists and students of literature each have an interest. Perhaps they may be especially helpful in working out the basic minimum. This may also be true of the even more intractable area of 'integration'. Again, students who had failed to integrate any of their learning in the ways described should be easy enough to recognize. Clearly, too, one should not pitch the requirement very high, since few are going to achieve the maturity that comes through integration while they are still completing their formal education. But school-leavers must at least be aware of what integration is in its different forms; beyond this, they must also provide evidence that they are not only aware of it but see its importance and are beginning to apply it to their own lives. All this, I am aware, is very embryonic. This whole area is one in which, to my knowledge, very little work has yet been done. But there could hardly be a more important topic to which educationists could address themselves.

If experts in different fields can work out basic minima in this way, we can then have a yardstick by which to ensure that every pupil has received an adequate education. This does not necessarily imply a school-leaving examination for everyone, based on these minima. If, for instance, a pupil can solve problems in calculus and the basic minimum in mathematics falls below the level of calculus, this itself is enough to show that he has reached the minimum. This can be generalized for all curriculum areas: work which shows a more advanced understanding than that minimally required is as good a test as any. In many fields it may even well be the best, e.g. where conventional examinations are ill able to discriminate real understanding from learning-off (and are in other well-known ways imperfect). It is surprising, perhaps, that this form of assessment – what might be called 'assessment by more advanced understanding' – is not, to my knowledge, widely used. But perhaps it is not so surprising, after all, in a society where forms of assessment are seen as competitive devices. For it only makes sense when one's objective is to ensure that those assessed have all reached the same standard rather than to see what is the best that each individual can do. Examinations of the more conventional kind may also, of course, be used to satisfy the first of these objectives, but just when and where they are preferable to assessment by more advanced understanding is a question for more detailed research.

Once one has fixed the basic minima in depth and breadth for the seventeen- or eighteen-year-old school leaver, one can proceed to work out syllabuses at different levels to lead pupils to them. There is no reason to think that any one syllabus will be the best for all children: there may be many routes to the same goal and different syllabuses may suit different children or different teachers (Hirst and Peters, 1970, pp. 69-70). On the other hand, diversity should not be so extreme as to make it impossible, practically speaking, to integrate the work of teachers in any one curriculum area through the different age-groups. The foundations of mathematical understanding laid by the teacher of seven-year-olds must support what is taught to eight-, nine- and ten-year-olds and so on until they reach the basic minimum. If there is no official syllabus extending through this age-range, there must at least be integration at school or individual level, so that the teacher of very young children clearly sees how her work locks in with that of her successors to lead up to the basic minimum. Without this integration, education becomes a hit-and-miss affair. If there is to be no public syllabus, there must at least be some kind of public check that syllabuses are properly integrated through time. The absence of such a check in our present educational system is, in my opinion, one of its most serious faults. What the best forms of public check might be and to what extent they would necessitate controls on the individual teacher's freedom to teach what he wants are again questions for research.

Compulsory and voluntary activities

Basic minima are features of a compulsory curriculum. In discussing which curriculum areas should be compulsory, I have largely concentrated on those activities which are unintelligible without participation. The case for these is unarguable: without participation one can gain no understanding of them and so will be cut off from them as options. But what of those other familiar timetable items – foreign languages, painting, games, cookery, handicraft and so on – about which I may have seemed so far somewhat lukewarm? I have argued that there is not the same reason as before for making them compulsory: they can be understood to some extent without participation. As I stressed, however, there may well be other reasons for insisting on them, although I know of no compelling ones. The onus is on those who wish to make them obligatory to argue their case afresh. This is an important point. It is still taken as read in many quarters, especially in our secondary modern schools, that the average child's education will be largely based on activities like these: this proposition has been indoctrinated into teachers so diligently for seventy odd years that it is now become the unquestioned first axiom of a whole belief system. But it is not at all self-evident. On the contrary: there seems no good reason why any of these activities should be compulsory. This is why their supporters must be challenged at every point to give their reasons.

Suppose, however, that good reasons are not available. It would not follow that these activities should not be taught at all. Not all learning need be compulsory. There is also room for voluntary activities: not optional ones which appear on timetables already, for these are only options within a compulsory framework; but activities which children are free to choose or not choose as they wish: in a voluntary system, opting out of the whole programme is

Why not have voluntary at home?

itself an option. The case for a voluntary system running parallel with the compulsory one is that children are not merely educands: they are also persons with their own life to lead. Adult life is typically differentiated into an area of compulsion – the work one has to do, the enforced roles one has to fill – and one of freedom or leisure. Adults can typically choose between many different leisure activities: they earn money which enables them, *inter alia*, and to different degrees, to follow activities of their choice. If this pattern is acceptable for adults, as I believe it is, I see no reason why it should not also be so for children. The compulsory curriculum which children might follow would be their equivalent of their parents' paid employment. Beyond this, they should be provided with the material wherewithal, within reason, to follow activities of their choice. There is a strong case here for providing them with institutions where all kinds of voluntary activities can go on, activities, unlike those in the compulsory system, about which children can understand enough to enable them to choose them as options. They will include not only the kind of things mentioned above, but also activities from the compulsory curriculum of which children have some understanding and wish to pursue at greater length.

A pattern for such a voluntary system is, with certain important reservations, the Young Pioneer movement found in eastern Europe.[2] In these countries, compulsory education is in principle in the morning only. Children are left free in the afternoon to join, if they want to, the various Pioneer 'circles' or groups, organized either on the school premises or in Pioneer Houses and Palaces serving several schools. These are elaborate youth centres, housing a great variety of 'circles' which go in for anything from gymnastics to model railways, to keeping pets, practical chemistry and playing the violin.

Eastern Europe is well ahead of us in voluntary education and I believe it has a lot to teach us. This is not to advocate slavish imitation. Voluntary education should not be used as a means of indoctrinating children into a set of political beliefs, as the Young Pioneer movement undoubtedly is. But even here we have something to learn. For the communists mix with their indoctrination a great deal of what for us would be worth-while moral education of a practical sort. Habits of co-operativeness and social service, as well as obedience to party and fatherland, are deliberately fostered through group activities.

A voluntary system in this country could find room for all the types of activity whose place in the compulsory curriculum is open to doubt. Children would be able to learn languages if they wanted to; draw, paint, sing, write stories, play instruments; do woodwork, cooking and needlework; play games, swim and do gymnastics; 'contract in' to religious groups. Community service could also find a place here. There would also be room, as in the Soviet system, to pursue all sorts of hobbies, from aeromodelling to building radios. The Newsom Report did well to stress these activities, but unfortunately still within an overall compulsory framework. If we ignore this framework, the voluntary education system I have in mind would be in many ways the realization of the Newsom ideal.

It should also satisfy the libertarians. For the strong point of those who favour maximum freedom is that the child is not simply an adult in the making. He is also a child, with his own life to lead, who should be left free to do what he wants as far as possible.

But, is freedom gun?

This means, of course, that once the compulsory part of the school day is over, the child has the right to do nothing, if he wants to; and some people may be horrified at the prospect of millions of children idle and uncontrolled. But there should be no shortage of volunteers. The attractiveness to children of such a voluntary system would be likely to make the real problem how to keep up with the numbers. No doubt there would be some children who did not want to join in. But provided one made sure they knew what activities were going on – which might mean more active encouragement for the younger than for the older child to attend – I see no reason for obstructing them in their wish not to join.

Many schools are moving in this direction. But too many children are still obliged to do things which they should not be obliged to; and too many lack the facilities and time to do all sorts of things they want to. Our education system needs to be rationalized. The compulsory element in it needs strengthening – to ensure that all children and not only the more able of them gain a thorough understanding of the basic disciplines. And the voluntary element needs not so much to be strengthened, as to be introduced, for we have very little conception of it as yet.

If it were introduced, it might well lead us to challenge another deep-lying assumption. It seems to have been taken as read since state education began a century ago that children should not only begin compulsory school at five, but also spend the whole of the school day, morning and afternoon, in compulsory activities (including options within a compulsory framework). But what are the grounds for this? I know of none. Again, the onus is on those who wish to support such a system to produce their arguments: *prima facie*, it seems morally unjustified, as an unfounded interference with the liberty of the child. In earlier chapters I have tried to indicate what kinds of compulsion can be justified. But I have said nothing about how much of the child's time, both from day to day and from year to year, should be spent this way. It may well be that compulsory activities need only occupy two or three hours a day on average: for all I know – or anyone knows – children may

Assumption

71

be able to spend the larger part of the day on voluntary activities. This is not a statement of belief. We quite simply have never got round to thinking seriously about this topic. The same is true of what should happen year by year. Is there any good reason why compulsory education should begin at five? Perhaps a better age would be seven. Or should there be very little compulsion on the younger child? Would it be better to leave as much as possible to adolescence? Until much more research has been done on all this and also on the amount of time a child needs, on average, to reach the basic minimum in different areas, we can only continue to grope on in the dark.

6

Forms of knowledge

This chapter is a long overdue acknowledgment of the debt I owe to P. H. Hirst's now classic curriculum theory expounded in his 'Liberal Education and the Nature of Knowledge' (1965) as well as in two further elaborations of it, by R. F. Dearden (1968) and P. H. Hirst and R. S. Peters (1970). Much of what was written in chapter 3 about category I activities is very similar to what these authors have written about 'forms of knowledge' (or forms of understanding). There seems to be a common thread running through both theories: that there are certain phenomena (category I activities in the one case, forms of knowledge in the other) of which one can have no conception without engaging in them and that education must be importantly concerned with these. To this extent the present theory is merely derivative. On the other hand, there are certain difficulties, often more of detail than of substance, in the 'forms of knowledge' theory in its different variations: what I hope to do in this section is to show how these difficulties can be removed, so that the strengths of the theory are revealed more clearly. The difficulties range themselves under three heads: (1) formulation, (2) justification, (3) completeness.

Formulation

Hirst's four criteria for picking out the forms of knowledge are as follows:

(1) They each involve certain central concepts that are peculiar to the form. For example, those of gravity, acceleration, hydrogen and photosynthesis characteristic of the sciences; number, integral, and matrix in mathematics; God, sin and predestination in religion; right, good and wrong in moral knowledge.

(2) In a given form of knowledge these and other concepts that denote, if perhaps in a very complex way, certain aspects of ex-

perience, form a network of possible relationships in which experience can be understood. As a result, the form has a distinctive logical structure ...

(3) The form, by virtue of its particular terms and logic, has expressions or statements that in some way or other, however indirect it may be, are testable against experience ...

(4) The forms have developed particular techniques and skills for exploring experience and testing their distinctive expressions ...

These criteria yield, in the Archambault article, the following forms of knowledge: mathematics, physical sciences, human sciences, history, religion, literature and the fine arts, philosophy, moral knowledge. There is considerable overlap between these and the category I activities of chapter 3: in both we find mathematics, physical science, the arts and philosophy. There are also differences: communication is a category I activity but not a form of knowledge; history, the human sciences, religion and moral knowledge are forms of knowledge but not category I activities. The reasons for this should become clearer as we proceed.

If we concentrate on the items which overlap, we recognize in both theories an emphasis here on conceptual barriers. The first two criteria of a form of knowledge refer to distinctive concepts and conceptual networks; and it is because category I activities bring with them concepts unintelligible to those who do not engage in them that they are in this category.

At this point I feel one should make a distinction which is not sufficiently stressed in the forms of knowledge theory, between two different sorts of conceptual barriers. Some barriers are more general than others. Mathematics introduces one to hundreds of new concepts – matrix, limit, cubic equation, cosine, etc. It is this wall of concepts – tightly interrelated, hierarchically arranged – which must be surmounted, or at least partially climbed, before one can grasp what mathematics is about. But not all activities in category I have such walls of concepts. Appreciation of the arts is an example. There are aesthetic concepts, like elegance, garishness, etc., but they do not form a close-knit system. It is the concept of art itself rather than any subordinate concepts which constitutes the wall in this case. Similarly with philosophy: what counts as philosophy is here the main obstacle.

It is important to make this distinction since one may be tempted to think that studying any discipline requires penetrating structures or networks of interrelated concepts as in physics or mathematics. This may lead one to bend aesthetic education in particular too much in a theoretical direction, weakening its specifically aesthetic character. Bruner (1960, p. 24), for instance, in discussing the appli-

74

cation of his theory of structure to literature, stresses the importance of coming to see novels as instances of – non-aesthetic – concepts (e.g. *Moby Dick* as a study of the theme of evil); whereas it is surely more important from an aesthetic point of view to see a work as a unique and irreplaceable particular.

The point just made, that aesthetic education is not essentially a theoretical matter, prompts a more general remark about the expression 'form of knowledge' as used in the theory. It is in some ways odd to call art a form of knowledge. There is no strain at all in using this term to describe mathematics or physical science or philosophy. Each of these disciplines is a pursuit of knowledge of one kind or another. Some artistic activities are also so classifiable, literary history and certain types of criticism, for instance. But others, like aesthetic contemplation, performance and other types of criticism aim rather at aesthetic experience. Here the picture becomes complicated because some would claim that intense aesthetic experience reveals knowledge of a different sort, about oneself, perhaps, or the deeper structure of reality. But this is only one kind of theory of aesthetic experience, and not one which one is constrained to accept. In old-fashioned terms, the pursuit of Beauty is a different kind of endeavour from the pursuit of Truth: they are better not brought under the same rubric. If to these we add the pursuit of Goodness, the point is reinforced; morality is not a form of knowledge: its aim is right action, not merely right belief. In so far as the 'forms of knowledge' theory is about directing pupils towards Truth, Beauty and Goodness, the word 'knowledge' is better dropped or qualified. In later versions of the theory it is: Dearden talks of 'forms of understanding' and Hirst and Peters of 'modes of experience and knowledge'.

This terminological difficulty is less important than the more substantial one that follows. The theory falls uneasily between two stools, or, rather, between two classifications. (a) The first classification is a logical or epistemological one, of separate families of concepts, each of which contains its own truth-criteria for propositions in which these concepts occur. We tell that an action is (morally) good according to different criteria from those employed in telling that a substance is hydrogen or from those employed that a vase is graceful. (There may be difficulties in establishing the objectivity of these criteria, but I need not go into those here). (b) The second classification is of academic pursuits or disciplines: mathematics, literature and the fine arts, history, philosophy, etc.

The forms of knowledge theory try to draw a distinction between those academic subjects which are independent disciplines (like mathematics) and those which are not (like geography) by making the hallmark of an independent discipline its unique one-to-one correlation with an item in list (a) i.e. with a specific and irreducible conceptual family. Geography then would not count as an independent discipline because it uses both mentalistic concepts (in referring to the intentions of such and such groups of people) and physicalistic concepts (like moraine and rift-valley). In the most recent formulation of the theory (Hirst and Peters, 1970, ch. 4), this logical priority of classification (a) over classification (b) becomes even clearer. A difficulty with the original formulation in the Archambault volume is that while history and the human sciences appear in the list as separate 'forms', it is not easy to identify any concepts which are peculiar to history and not to, say, psychology or sociology. On the other hand, as mentioned above, history and the human sciences use mentalistic concepts (e.g. motive) which are not used in mathematics or natural science. In the 'Logic of Education' list, accordingly, history and the human sciences do not appear as such. There is, instead, a form of understanding whose subject-matter is our own and others' minds. This is clearly distinguished, for instance, from that concerned with knowledge of the sensible world. This last is a distinction at the level of classification (a), between the family of mentalistic concepts – believing, hoping, intending, seeing, etc. – and that of concepts applicable to the sensible world – red, cloud, hydrogen, heat, etc. (Other 'forms' in the more recent list are, as before, formal logic and mathematics, moral, religious, aesthetic and philosophical understanding.)

Conceptual schemes, therefore, have a priority in the theory over academic disciplines. The thesis is that a liberal education should be an initiation into all the different mutually irreducible conceptual schemes. But this creates a serious difficulty. It would seem that one could be liberally educated without knowing any history or science, for instance. For as regards 'knowledge of minds', one could acquire a very adequate grasp of mental concepts, even the more sophisticated of them, from one's ordinary social intercourse. One does not need history, psychology or any other academic discipline to be adept in this area. And if we turn to 'physicalistic' concepts we see the same picture. I use the term 'physicalistic' rather tentatively, since one of the problems which the theory has to face is how to characterize that conceptual area which corresponds to natural science. In the texts mentioned, it is simply referred to as the area of 'physical science'. But since the theory claims that its 'forms' are exhaustive at least at this point in time, i.e. there are now no other independent conceptual schemes than the ones it picks out, there are many concepts of a quite ordinary sort which do not seem to fit unless we broaden the area of physical science. Concepts like 'force', 'mass', 'atom' clearly fall under the latter, but what of such homely concepts as 'milk-shake', 'hot water bottle', 'sticky', 'hot' or, indeed, most of the concepts we use to describe sensible things and their properties? One is faced with a dilemma. On the one hand one could broaden the area of physical science into an area of 'physicalistic' concepts.[1] But if one does this, a child could be initiated into this wider area simply by learning its mother tongue and without ever being acquainted with physical science. Even a child of five or six can use innumerable concepts to describe the sensible world; and with these concepts, of course, comes some understanding of the particular truth-criteria appropriate to them. If, however, one insists that a scientific understanding is a *sine qua non* of a liberal education, then one has to draw a distinction between ordinary language concepts and the technical concepts of science, arguing that both areas must be mastered. The theory that there are six or seven conceptual areas, those of physical science, mathematics, the arts and so on, will have to be abandoned. Ordinary language provides another conceptual area outside these.

One objection to this might be that in ordinary language we see more sophisticated concepts in embryo: number-concepts form the basis of mathematics, just as concepts of natural kinds – colours, rocks, animals, metals – are stepping stones into science: the line which I have been stressing, between language and discipline, is not sharp but gradated. There are two points to make in reply to this. First, while it is true that science and mathematics must be anchored in ordinary language in this way, there is still a gap which ought to be stressed between them and it. One is not thinking mathematically when using number concepts for counting in everyday practical affairs, but only when one has begun to reflect on the relations between the numbers themselves: there is a jump here from practice to theory. Similarly with the exact sciences: these begin with the 'rape of the senses', with the abstraction from the sensible properties of things to the invisible relationships by which these observables are explained. Second, the web of ordinary language concepts cannot be parcelled out into embryo physical scientific concepts, embryo mathematical concepts, embryo aesthetic concepts and so on. For (i), some concepts, e.g. the 'practical' concepts like 'chair' or 'knife' mentioned in note 1 above, cannot be ascribed clearly to the embryo-physical-scientific domain since their definition must refer to the uses of what falls under them (chairs, knives, etc.) and hence include 'mentalistic' concepts about human intentions. (ii) Some ordinary language concepts are so pervasive that they enter into every other conceptual scheme and hence cannot be ascribed to any. These are formal concepts, like the concepts of 'thing' and 'property', 'truth' and 'fact'. Concepts too like 'time' and 'space' are also framework-concepts of language in general, belonging to physical science no more than they do to mathematics, music or painting. Concepts like these cannot be ascribed to the different 'forms of knowledge'. In so far as the theory claims that its 'forms' are exhaustive of all the concepts there are, it falls short at this point. The solution is frankly to recognize that ordinary language resists being engulfed into the 'forms'. It is a phenomenon on its own. This is why, in the theory presented in chapter 3 above, it comes out as a category I activity on a par with others.

So much, then, for some of the difficulties in formulating the 'forms of knowledge' theory. The main one is the poor fit between academic disciplines and putative primordial conceptual areas. There is even some danger here, paradoxically perhaps, that in putting the theory into educational practice the crucial importance of mastering these disciplines as a means to autonomy may receive less recognition than it should. For the more one stresses the continuity of the disciplines with ordinary language, the harder it is to deny that a child who has merely acquired a good stock of ordinary language concepts has been properly educated. In the interests of all our children, especially those liable to be given a secondary curriculum on the 'Newsom' pattern, where the disciplines are virtually non-existent, it is most important to resist this move. It is for these reasons that it is better to emphasize the discontinuity of the disciplines, by translating the forms of knowledge terminology into the terminology of category I and category II activities found in chapter 3.

Justification

Problems also arise over the justification of the thesis. Two kinds of justification have been put forward, a 'transcendental' one by Hirst and an instrumental one by R. F. Dearden.

(a) Hirst's argument (1965, p. 126) runs as follows:

> If the achievement of knowledge is necessarily the development
> of mind in its most basic sense, then it can readily be seen
> that to ask for a justification for the pursuit of knowledge is
> not at all the same thing as to ask for the justification for,
> say, teaching all children a foreign language or making them
> orderly and punctual in their behaviour. It is in fact a peculiar
> question asking for justification for any development of the
> rational mind at all. To ask for the justification of any form
> of activity is significant only if one is in fact committed
> already to seeking rational knowledge. To ask for a justification

of the pursuit of rational knowledge itself therefore presupposes some commitment to what one is seeking to justify.

This argument is valid in one way, but not in a way which supports the general thesis about a liberal education. It is true that there is something logically odd about asking the question, 'Why pursue rational knowledge?' If one asks this question, one is presumably pursuing knowledge: one wants to know why rational knowledge should be pursued. In asking 'Why?' one is, furthermore, asking for reasons – and so may be said to be seeking not merely knowledge but also – in so far as the adjective adds anything not already contained in the concept of knowledge – rational knowledge. In asking the question, therefore, one is already committed to what one is seeking to justify.

All this is quite true. But the argument does not support the prescription for a liberal education because it fails to show that there is something logically odd about asking whether or not one should 'pursue rational knowledge' in a rather stronger sense of this expression than the one just discussed. A theoretical physicist can be said to be 'pursuing rational knowledge' in this stronger sense: that is to say, he is engaged in the discovery of new truths, in finding out why things happen as they do. In asking the question, 'Why pursue rational knowledge?' in this sense, i.e.: 'Why pursue knowledge in different areas, scientific, historical, etc.?', one is not already committed to such a pursuit. One is indeed committed to wanting to know the answer to the question, but to nothing more than this.

It is clear that this justification is of the same logical form as that which Peters gives in support of 'worth-while activities' (see above, pp. 11 ff). In asking the question, 'Why pursue rational knowledge?' or the question, 'Why do this rather than that?' one is committed in a weak sense to the pursuit of rational knowledge (or the pursuit of truth). But then in asking any 'Why?' question, e.g., 'Why is the bus late?', one is equally so committed. Neither the man who asks Hirst's question nor the man who asks Peters's is committed to pursue or merely value academic disciplines. In both cases the questioners may be sceptics. It would be logically impossible, it would seem, for them to be committed.

(b) Dearden's justification (1968, p. 61) is that the different forms of understanding – mathematical, scientific, aesthetic, etc. – are 'basic constitutive elements in rational choice'. An instrumental reason would now seem to be available for initiating children into these forms: this initiation helps them to make rational choices, to choose their own paths through life and not simply do or believe what others tell them, in short, to become autonomous persons.

It is clear that this kind of justification is similar to the justification of category I activities which I gave above in chapter 3 and I would not so much disagree with it as argue that it needs filling out at two crucial points. (i) In what sense are the different forms of understanding 'basic constitutive elements in rational choice'? Dearden writes, in answer to this question (1968, p. 79):

> Certainly it is not being claimed that all our knowledge belongs to one or other of these forms of understanding. Primitive physical abilities, such as the knowledge of how to raise one's arm, or locate one's sensations, are not included. Nor is a great deal of our perceptual and memory knowledge. We do not need a formal education to enable us to see birds and houses, to remember what we did yesterday, or to recognise at least the simpler sorts of motivation in other people.
>
> What is being claimed is that the forms of understanding above mentioned are basic ways in which human experience has, as a matter of fact, been extended and elaborated in the course of history. Such understanding is therefore presupposed by rational choice and hence is of great relevance to formal education, of which it is in special need for its transmission.

He goes on to add that 'all but the simplest kinds of human activity draw upon these forms of understanding', instancing vocational activities, like teaching or technology, and leisure activities, like aqualung diving.

It is true that in order to make rational choices of many activities one needs various forms of understanding. But it still needs to be shown why science, history and so on have any more important a place on the curriculum than, say, Latin or cookery. Just as mathematics opens doors to vocational and leisure activities, so does Latin. It is admitted that not all our knowledge belongs to one or other of the 'forms'. Knowing how to raise one's arm, for instance, or knowing that something is a house are also in a sense types of knowledge; but they are not considered further, on the grounds that a formal education is not necessary to acquire them. But how far is this argument applicable to Latin? Assuming that a 'formal education' is one where one has to engage in courses of study under the direction of a teacher and cannot simply pick things up informally, few would doubt that a formal education is necessary to learn Latin. In so far as the forms of understanding owe their pre-eminence in the curriculum to the fact that a formal education is needed for their transmission, they would seem thus far to be on a par with Latin. The argument, I suggest, needs to be modified somewhat. The crucial point is not what is necessary for the transmission of X but what is necessary for understanding the kind of thing X is. Transmitting a knowledge of Latin may well necessitate a formal education. But Latin still lacks the curricular status of subjects like mathematics or the arts because it is possible to understand something of what it is to speak or write in Latin without learning how to do this – while it is impossible to understand what it is to think mathematically without learning how to. This part of the account, in short, would require more explicit supplementation by the kind of argument for category I activities presented in earlier chapters.

(ii) The second crux of the argument is the discussion of autonomy. If one grants that one must be initiated into various forms of understanding in order to become an autonomous person, a complete justification of this curriculum requires a justification of autonomy as an ideal. This is given in Dearden's chapter 3, pp. 46-9. The autonomous man is here described as one whose beliefs and actions are not based on what authorities dictate but on one's own rational assessment. Two arguments are provided as a justification for this ideal. (a) 'Even for me to question whether I ought to test my beliefs and make my choices according to my own reasoned judgment, rather than in obedience to authorities, is already to have decided in favour of autonomy; for I am asking for *reasons* as to what I ought to do, and taking it for granted that it is *I* who will decide the merits of the answers' (p. 46). This is another 'transcendental' argument, rather like those already discussed by Peters and Hirst; and, like these, it is not strong enough to support the value-conclusion it contains. In this case the value-conclusion is a commitment to, a decision in favour of, autonomy. But the argument only entitles one to conclude that in asking the question 'Ought I to be autonomous?' one is *ipso facto* an autonomous person: only an autonomous person can seriously ask this question. This may be true, but it does not show that the questioner must value his autonomy. Suppose, for instance, he is wondering whether to remain an autonomous person or to become an unquestioning adherent of some religious faith: he can autonomously ask his question and still come down in favour of the latter. Some men who go off to live in monasteries do just this: autonomy is a burden for anyone and for some the time comes when the burden is no longer worth bearing. (b) The second justification of autonomy consists of four further reasons: '(i) that through it we can achieve integrity and thus not be involved in self-deception, or the deception of others; (ii) that it permits us to develop an intelligible and well-grounded knowledge of our true situation in the world; (iii) that it permits and encourages us, in that situation, to pursue the good as we ourselves judge it, though correspondingly it makes us personally responsible for our choices; (iv) that consistency with its own principles already requires that we be fair in our dealings with others' (p. 47). Dearden recognizes that one may raise questions about the further justification of these values, 'for unless they are justified further are they not simply arbitrary commitments?' His reply is that 'no-one could *understand* what was meant by independence, integrity, freedom of choice and so on without also seeing that each of them had features such as could well make it highly prized' (p. 47). Suppose for the sake of argument we grant this point about understanding: we are only granting that to understand what e.g. freedom of choice is we have to understand why it could well be highly prized. But what some may prize highly others may reject. Even if to understand what freedom of choice is I must understand why others may value it, I could still disvalue it myself. Whether or not one values autonomy and its attendant ideals is perhaps, after all, a subjective matter. Perhaps one cannot produce any valid argument to show that one must value it as an ideal of life. But if there is no such argument one cannot justify giving children a curriculum whose rationale is in terms of the autonomy ideal: one will be open to the charge of basing one's curriculum on what is, after all, merely a subjective preference.

The way out of the justification problem at this point is, as I suggested earlier in chapter 2, to distinguish between ideals of education and ideals of life. Autonomy as an ideal of life may simply be a matter of individual preference. But it still may be the case that educators must aim at making all their pupils autonomous, for the reasons given in chapter 2. Whether once the pupil becomes autonomous he chooses to remain autonomous is his own affair – at least, as far as only his own good is in question: I say a little more on this below, pp. 84-7.

Completeness

Comments on the incompleteness of the forms of knowledge theory as a theory of the curriculum will be very brief, as most of the positive points have already been covered in chapters 3 and 4. The main lacuna is that the very important stress on the differentiation of forms of understanding into different areas needs to be complemented by an equally important stress on one's integration of what one learns into a total pattern of life. It is true that the version of the theory in Hirst and Peters (1970) stresses the importance of an 'adequate education in the making of practical, and especially moral, judgments' (p. 72), which requires the integration of knowledge from diverse areas. This latter integration is wider in range than the type just mentioned and may even not include it.

It seems largely to be concerned with something less global, with being able to make adequate moral or prudential judgments in the kinds of problem situations that repeatedly confront one. While not wishing to deny the importance of this as an educational objective, it seems to me that there is still something lacking: a man might have a good understanding of the different forms of knowledge for their own sake, be sensitive in his day to day moral judgments, efficient in the organization of his personal life, and still not have reflected on the overall pattern of his life. He might throw himself for some time into the pursuit of mathematics for its own sake, switch to an equally absorbed hour or two with Keats, and so on through the disciplines; but he might never have reflected on these elements in a total pattern of life which he had constructed for himself. A 'culture-vulture', so this criticism would run, is not properly speaking an educated person. In Plato's image, he would be still a prisoner in the cave, blindly following each of his cultural hobbies and never able to discover the One, the unifying principle which would connect the many parts of his disconnected existence into some kind of harmony; or in Kierkegaard's terms, he would still be at the stage of 'aesthetic' existence, unaware as yet of the 'ethical' life which lay above (1843).

Curriculum theories which favour an initiation into different 'forms of knowledge' are incomplete in that they concentrate on the 'chunks' which pupils must acquire – admittedly ways of understanding rather than the old strings of words, but 'chunks' all the same – and thus run this risk, unless supplemented by some integrative principle, of producing merely cultured rather than educated men. True, the different 'chunks' are not completely discrete. In Hirst's scheme, for instance, two of the 'forms of knowledge' which form the basis of the theory are physical science and mathematics. Here the former makes use of the latter: they are interconnected to this extent. But interconnection of this sort clearly falls short of the ideal of integration described in the last paragraph: one could grasp this kind of interconnection without having reflected on the shape of one's life as a whole.

From this point of view certain forms of thought included in the original 'forms of knowledge' list attain a new prominence. Religion and history are in this class. These do not fit neatly into the 'forms' classification. History is a kind of knowledge, but not strictly a 'form of knowledge' as defined, since there are no unique historical concepts. Religion may be misconstrued as a kind of knowledge in any sense. I am not talking about theology here, but about the religious way of life: this may be based on faith rather than knowledge. Since in order to 'integrate' their life in the present sense, students will have to understand different ways of life as well as

But Hirst said 'forms were all there was to education

different isolable activities, some kind of religious education is essential at this point. Some historical understanding is important for the same reason: there is no need to repeat the arguments already sketched in chapters 3 and 4.

Two final points on the incompleteness of the theory, both again already mentioned. The first is its inadequacy on the practical side of the curriculum. This comes out in several ways, often differently in various versions of the theory. In the original account (Hirst, 1965) there was no need to emphasize the practical, since the educational objective was the acquisition of knowledge for its own sake. The 'human sciences' were seen here as intrinsically interesting: their instrumental functions were not relevant. Hirst's and Peters's later version (1970) paid more attention to the practical, as we saw above: children had to be adequately educated in making practical, especially moral judgments. To do this, they had to bring the different forms of knowledge to bear on different practical problems. But, as we have seen, (a) forms of practical understanding like economics and political science fit ill into a 'forms of knowledge' scheme; and (b) the importance of such practical understanding in helping one to work out one's preferred pattern of life is overlooked.

The second point is that the 'forms of knowledge' theory is incomplete in its 'democratization' of the 'forms'. There is no reason within the theory why any form is any more important, educationally speaking, than another. But if the argument in chapter 5 is valid, the humanities have a certain priority over both the natural and the social sciences in that they have a special contribution to make in helping to open up different ways of life and to 'integrate' in the sense described.

As a final point it is also worth remarking on the oddness of including 'moral understanding' in a list of the 'forms' as if it were on a par with mathematical or any other 'form'. Moral understanding, as Plato rightly saw in the *Republic*, is on a higher plane than other kinds: why this is so should be clear enough from the paramount place among educational objectives given to moral integration in chapter 4.

Equipment or permanence?

It may well be objected that the previous discussion of the 'forms of knowledge' theory fails to do it justice. I have made it seem too much like the theory of category I activities, without stressing one important respect in which it goes beyond this. In the category I theory the emphasis has been on equipping the individual student to choose his own way of life. This emphasis is also prominent in

Dearden's version of the forms of knowledge theory. But there is another line of thought running through not only Dearden's, but also through Hirst's and Peters's accounts which needs to be isolated. This is that the forms of knowledge are not merely equipment for a certain purpose, but, more importantly, permanent mental acquisitions. Equipment can be jettisoned once it has served its purpose: once a man has chosen, say, the life of the creative artist, there may be no reason as far as his own interests are concerned, why he should not forget all his mathematics – not only the details, but, if this were possible, even his understanding of what kind of an activity mathematical thinking is. The forms of knowledge theory, however, requires a continued understanding of the different forms. Mental development is from no understanding, or, at best, a confused understanding, to a clear grasp of what differentiates the various forms of thought. This is mental maturity. Once one has reached the ideal, one should retain it: the artist who forgets his mathematics has slid back a step.

Intuitively, the forms of knowledge theory seems to be right over this issue: a rational education is not simply about equipment for choice, but about the development of more permanent dispositions. But can one give substance to this intuition? What reasons can be adduced to support the 'permanence' as distinct from the 'equipment' view?

One appeal may be to the interests of the individual. Choice of a way of life is not a once-for-all matter. One never knows how one's choices may alter in the future. It is prudent, therefore, to retain some understanding of the different forms of thought in case this happens. The artist is stupid to let slip his mathematical understanding since his choice of future options will be limited.

It is important to see that this is not an argument for the intrinsic worth of different forms of thought. They are not a necessary part of the 'Good for man' where this refers only to ends; the argument is that they are good for man in another way – as dispositions which he must foster so as to avoid possible harm in the future.

How valid is this argument, if universally applied? Suppose one applies it to a man who is devoted to music in all its forms and knows that he has only a year to live. Must he, too, maintain an interest in mathematics or science, even though he has no inclination towards them? There would seem little point. But if we say this of him, have we any reason to say anything different about anyone else? If we were each sure of another five thousand years of life, it might well be prudent for us not to let our learning rust; but human life is short and its end usually unpredictable. If a man impressed by the shortness of life drops part of what he has

85

learnt for the sake of other things, who can say that he is less rational than the man who keeps all his learning in good trim, just in case ... ? Prudence of the latter kind is prudence to excess. It rests on an unrealistic picture of what human life is like. It underplays the role that conscious decision can play in the shaping of one's future, assuming, as it does, that something may always occur to cause one radically to alter one's way of life, that, say, a taste for deep-sea diving or cosmology may at any time sweep one aside from one's chosen path. Some men may wish, rather like the sceptic on empirical knowledge, to make their future secure against even such improbabilities as these; but no one is rationally constrained to follow them.

All this, of course, assumes that one can try to forget whole areas of learning. This may not be so easy as it sounds. One might forget the details of mathematics, but it might not be so easy to forget what kind of activity mathematical thinking is. This, I suppose (but I may be wrong on this), is an empirical issue. But suppose it turned out that, generally speaking, when people acquire an understanding of category I activities, the broad lines of this understanding remain as permanent mental acquisitions. On the arguments produced so far this result could not be shown to be good or bad in any objective sense. Some people might welcome it for themselves; for others, like the artist not interested in mathematics, it would be of no value, an ineradicable understanding which one could put to no use.

But whether or not such understanding is ineradicable there is an argument of a different kind to show that it ought to be a permanent mental possession. This is a moral argument. Whether or not it is in my interests to maintain an understanding of different forms of knowledge (or category I activities) it would certainly seem to be my moral duty to do so. If morality enjoins me to consider others' interests impartially with my own, I do not have any reason to think, as I may have in my own case, that the ends which others value will all fall within a certain range narrower than the total range of all possible ends. If I lose all my understanding of science I will lose my appreciation of what others see in scientific pursuits and be consequently less attentive to their wants. In other ways, too, a continued broad understanding of the disciplines is necessary to moral action: one cannot guarantee that a knowledge of science, for instance, will not be useful in furthering others' interests even though they themselves have not chosen science in any way as an end. This is true both at a personal level, in applying one's knowledge for the benefit of particular individuals, and also at a political level, where one's duty as a citizen may require one to judge on issues – pollution, for instance

– which depend partly on scientific data (P. A. White, 1971, pp. 21-4). The general argument in this paragraph explains the heavy qualification I have made at two previous points (pp. 23 and 82) to the claim that although educators should see to it that pupils become autonomous as a result of their education, whether they stay autonomous, i.e. whether they value autonomy as an ideal of life, is their own concern. From their own point of view, they may prefer to become slaves or true believers. The qualification resides in the 'from their own point of view'. For if one looks at things now from a moral point of view, the argument in this paragraph provides an excellent reason why one should not surrender one's autonomy to others. I would not go so far as to claim this principle as absolute (exception-less).

I have not laid much emphasis in this essay on the moral justification of curriculum activities. This has been because I have been especially concerned with working out the implications of looking at the curriculum from the point of view of an individual's interests alone. The moral justifications would need another essay at least as long as this one. (One should note, incidentally, that the moral justification given in the last paragraph does not concern only the compulsory curriculum activities we have been describing. It is wider in scope. For there is the same moral reason to retain one's understanding of other activities – of games, for instance, or practical skills – as to retain one's understanding of science or art.) It is important to stress again the serious incompleteness of the theory presented in the bulk of this essay. It is not enough to abstract an individual from the moral world in which he must live and consider his education from the viewpoint of his own interests alone. As a moral being he cannot be content with this restricted view. An abstraction useful as a means of classifying the nature of educational ends must be abandoned when one looks at things more broadly.

7

Some objections

A number of objections may well be made to the position sketched so far.

Objection 1. 'The argument has consisted largely of rationalizations supporting a traditional curriculum taught in a traditional way. It lays too much emphasis on knowledge and too little on the personal and emotional development of the child. It seems to by-pass much of the recent work in freeing curricula from their traditional shackles: in particular it takes for granted conventional subject divisions and ignores moves towards integrated or interdisciplinary courses.'

There are a number of points here. First, the curriculum suggested has not at all been traditional for all children. It is something like a traditional grammar school curriculum, but even here the differences are as great as the similarities. In particular, there is none of the grammar school emphasis on compulsory languages or compulsory games; knowledge of ways of life and the development of a personal *Weltanschauung* are stressed as much as knowledge of the disciplines; work is structured so as to lead up to a basic minimum and not to competitive examinations. Second, and I must stress this point, very little has been said so far about the way in which curriculum items should be taught. Nothing, in particular, has been said in favour of 'traditional methods', in so far as this phrase brings to mind the stereotype of a teacher standing in front of his class, instructing or questioning largely passive pupils. All sorts of teaching methods are compatible with the theory. Which are preferable is a part-empirical, part-moral question that I shall not broach here. There is certainly no presumption in favour of the 'traditional' approach. Misunderstanding may also arise here from the emphasis throughout on 'compulsion'. In arguing that a child should be compelled to reach a certain standard in, say, science, I have meant only that it is not up to him whether or not he studies science: he cannot be allowed to skip it. I have not meant that he should be driven to study it, e.g. by fear of punishment. Compulsion is not coercion: the gentlest of methods is compatible with a compulsory system. Third, it is only true in one sense of the term that this curriculum emphasizes 'knowledge'. It certainly stresses the importance of coming to know what different activities and ways of life involve. But it does not particularly stress the pursuit of knowledge in the sense of the theoretical disciplines. Aesthetic and moral development, for instance, are no less prominent. Still less does this theory advocate the acquisition of 'knowledge' where this means memorized material: it is hard to see how this could lead one towards the kinds of understanding required. Fourth, while welcoming many of the recent moves to liberalize curricula, there are one or two things to say about the current pleas to 'break down subject barriers' in favour of 'integrated' courses.

An 'integrated' curriculum is often said to respect the fact that knowledge is a 'seamless whole', not something chopped up into bits and pieces. Without launching on a wholesale critique of this position, let me restrict myself to pointing out that, taken one way, this notion of 'integration' is nonsensical. Learning mathematics is one thing, learning to appreciate poetry is another: they are distinguished by different intentions (the pursuit of truth in the one case and of beauty[1] in the other) and by their employment of different and mutually irreducible concepts (see chapter 6). Mathematics, similarly, is logically different from science and philosophy: ignoring or blurring these logical distinctions can only help to prevent children from getting inside these disciplines. (Which, to a cynic, might suggest one reason why this notion of 'integration' has been so popular in some quarters.) Knowledge, therefore, is not a 'seamless whole'. There may or may not be a case for teaching the different sciences – physics, chemistry, biology – under the one rubric of 'general science': if 'integration' only goes as far as this, it is at least binding together disciplines which have important structural features in common. But in so far as it goes beyond this to pulp everything together, it is unintelligible. Being educated must consist, to some extent, in learning isolated bits and pieces. This is not to say that it must consist in learning isolated facts – propositions of history, biology and so on which must be stored and reproduced to order. Part of the impetus towards 'integration' may have come from a well-justified reaction to this too-familiar tradition. 'Facts', if necessary, must find their place in larger patterns of thought: if one likes, they must be 'integrated' into them. But these larger patterns cannot themselves all be run together. One's achievements must come, to some extent, in isolable 'chunks'.

If, as suggested, there are logical barriers at some point between different disciplines, e.g. between art and mathematics, these are not the kinds of barriers that can be altered by human decisions. Not all subject-barriers are conventional. There is dangerous confusion on this point. In some quarters academic divisions, between different subjects, have come to be conflated in a curious way with social divisions, between different social classes. It is sometimes even suggested that the ruling classes have created subject-divisions to support their own social hegemony and that if social divisiveness is to disappear then curricular divisiveness must disappear with it. But this blurs the distinction between the logical and the conventional mentioned above. A curriculum chopped neatly into distinct subjects has been a feature of grammar and public school education and therefore more closely associated with the middle classes than with others. So much is true. It is also true that many of these divisions are conventional and could be altered. But it does not follow that all divisions are conventional. This, as I have pointed out, does not make sense. The drive to bulldoze all barriers away is dangerous because it directs reforming efforts away from ensuring that all children learn the arts, sciences, mathematics and so on, essential for their personal autonomy and moral development. Curiously, the social revolutionary and the social conservative find themselves now on the same side of the fence. As so often happens in educational debate, those who support the social status quo often adopt policies which can come to seem very enlightened.

Objection 2. 'The theory lays too much emphasis on extrinsic values, on career-choice, for instance. Education is essentially a matter of initiating one into worth-while activities pursued for their own sake. In so far as things are taught and learned for extrinsic reasons they are not properly to be called educational activities at all. (On the other hand, some activities which are pursued for extrinsic ends, like carpentry or cookery, may also be educationally worth while in so far as they also have intrinsic value.)'

There do not seem to be any good reasons why education should exclude extrinsic values. Given that education must, among other things, be in the child's own interests, it is in his interests not only to be aware of the kinds of things he may pursue for their intrinsic value: he must also have some understanding, as emphasized in chapter 4, about how these ends may be achieved, through career-choices and in other ways. It is certainly true that a proper education must not fail to stress intrinsic ends, and a weaker way of interpreting this objection is to take it as saying just this. But there seems little to be said for its stronger interpretation, that education should be concerned only with the intrinsic.

Nevertheless, feeling against extrinsic values runs high in educational circles, and not only in the pages of educational theory. It may be useful to spend a moment or two suggesting why this might be. Here are two suggestions. (A) Curriculum activities may be seen as intrinsically or extrinsically valuable from (a) the pupil's point of view, or (b) the teacher's or the school's. Distaste for extrinsic values is often reasonable when it comes from those who are looking at things from the pupil's point of view. For the pupil can see his algebra-learning, for instance, either as something intrinsically fascinating, or as something which he has to do in order to please his teacher or his parents or keep his overall position at the top of the class. The ideal is that he comes to love algebra for its own sake: as long as he views his studies in this area simply as means to further ends, he is not properly inside the subject. But a preference for intrinsic motivation from the pupil's point of view is not incompatible with stressing extrinsic as well as intrinsic values from the teacher's point of view. For the teacher knows, as the child does not – or not at first – that a knowledge of algebra is important in physical science, the technologies which spring from this, and the careers which are centred on these technologies. From the teacher's point of view, or perhaps more exactly, from the point of view of the school as an institution, there would be no reason to teach algebra only for its intrinsic values, although these must surely form a part of the reason for teaching it.

This is one possible explanation, therefore, of a distaste for extrinsic values in education: one may be looking at things from the point of view of the pupil, not the institution. (But even here, while intrinsic motivation is obviously all-important when a pupil is beginning to get on the inside of a subject, once he is well on the way he must also be led to see the extrinsic reasons for studying it, i.e. he must come gradually to see the rationale for his studies that his school has worked out. At this level, points of view (a) and (b) coalesce.)

(B) A second possible explanation is concerned not with pupils' motivation but with the aims of the schools as institutions. In so far as curriculum activities are seen as providing 'tickets', passports to 'O' or 'A' level successes and then to higher education or such and such careers, they might well be said to be taught for extrinsic reasons. But the answer to the objection that an exclusive pursuit of 'tickets' is anti-educational is not that only intrinsic reasons will do. For there are extrinsic reasons and extrinsic reasons –

and not every kind is to be deplored. Suppose a school includes mathematics in its curriculum partly so as to open the door to engineering as a career: a knowledge of mathematics is not merely a ticket, replaceable by any other kind of knowledge, but a logically necessary condition of being an engineer, and as such quite irreplaceable.

Objection 3. 'A broad compulsory curriculum is out of place at the secondary stage. At primary school level there are certain subjects of outstanding importance which children must master if they are to maintain the means of communication within the society.' But the secondary school cannot aim at 'continuing the liberal education started in primary school ... The difficulty is that no general agreement exists as to what subjects make up the basis of a liberal education ... Perhaps adolescents should be given more freedom to choose the subjects they wish to study in accordance with their own aptitude and interests and not to meet the dictates of any pre-arranged curriculum. No doubt they should be encouraged to think also of the significance of such subjects to the future pattern of their lives.' Vocational guidance would help them to choose wisely. It should 'be concerned with individual choice of specialist subjects at an early stage of the secondary school course, as well as with the later stage of transition from school to work' (Vaughan, 1970, pp. 10-12).

Much of this argument is acceptable, given one assumption: that by the time they leave primary school children can reach the basic minimum for which I have been pressing. But if, as seems likely, the assumption is unfounded, the whole thesis falls to the ground. It may well be true that there is no general agreement about the content of a liberal education at secondary level. But it does not follow from this that one should introduce a 'cafeteria', counsellor-guided, system on the American pattern. Neither does it follow from the fact that there is no general agreement at present that there will be none in the future. This essay is indeed intended as one step along the road.

There are several objections to a cafeteria-curriculum. If children choose their own curricula, they cannot rationally choose them. At best they will be able to choose them as means to further ends, but only on authority. A child knowing nothing of science, for instance, might opt for a course in physics if he has been told that doing this will help him to get a good job. 'Physics' to him will be nothing but a name. In so far, then, as children are not choosing on authority (or purely at random), they will necessarily remain imprisoned among things they already know about.

If children choose on authority, then everything depends on how educationally enlightened the authority is. If the authority chooses a broad compulsory curriculum on the lines laid down in this essay that is unobjectionable, but the notion of a cafeteria-curriculum as an alternative to a pre-arranged compulsory one disappears. If the authority (parent, teacher, peer group or counsellor) chooses things which open the doors to 'good jobs', like maths or physics, but which the child knows only as names, there is no guarantee that the child will receive the broad education suggested in earlier sections: he may well be cut off from all kinds of options.

If we turn to a cafeteria system directed very largely by school-counsellors, as suggested in Objection 3, there are further reasons for scepticism. The 'educational and vocational' (E. and V.) counsellor who is currently finding a new home for himself on this side of the Atlantic is somewhat of a Janus figure.[2] It is not clear whether he is primarily the servant of the child, whose aim is to enlarge his vocational and cultural horizons, or primarily the servant of the industrial order, gentling children into careers and ways of life for which they are supposed to be fitted by 'aptitude and ability'. For a counselling system – I am not talking about its function in helping pupils with their personal problems, but with its E. and V. function – could well be an excellent means of preserving the essential features of the old eleven-plus regime when schools turn comprehensive. Like earlier devices – a maturationist educational theory or a 'practical' curriculum – it could help to keep down the numbers of the more highly educated.

But even if these insinuations are misplaced and the E. and V. counsellor is not intended to be a new agent of social control but a genuine promoter of the child's best interests, one thing is clear: he could only help the child to plan out his own curriculum if this curriculum were designed to reach something like the broad basic minima advocated here. Whether there would still be much call for the E. and V. counsellor if this condition were respected I do not know.

Objection 4. 'The reply to Objection 3 ignores the important point that a cafeteria system allows a child's individuality fully to express itself. The alternative "basic minimum" curriculum aims at uniformity. Imagine what it would be like if every child in the country followed it: millions upon millions of carbon-copy school leavers turned out each year by thousands of teaching factories, each one the facsimile of some central planner's blueprint. This would be to produce a nation of robots, not of individuals. Children are all different. We should respect these differences and centre our educational efforts around them, rather than try to cast everyone into the same mould.'

This is a familiar, *Daily Telegraph*, kind of argument. Really, though, it is not an argument at all, but propaganda. There is no reason to be alarmed by the word 'uniformity'.

One cannot rationally pronounce oneself for or against 'uniformity' until one knows in what respect people are said to be uniform. One may indeed object to living in a society where everyone shares exactly the same tastes and interests: where everyone, say, prefers blue curtains at their windows, spends two evenings a week playing bridge or listens only to eighteenth-century music. That would indeed be a carbon-copy society and, while not necessarily morally wrong if everyone indeed did want to do the same thing as others, it would not be a society which many would find congenial. But other kinds of uniformity are by no means abhorrent. No one would object to everyone's being uniformly honest or considerate, or press for the full development of individual differences in the area of truthfulness and untruthfulness. In the sphere of basic morality we expect everybody to be the same. We ought to expect everyone to receive the same basic education, for all the reasons already mentioned.

It is not true that uniformity of education provision entails the uniformity of a carbon-copy society. Once people have received their basic educational equipment, what they choose to do with it, as I have stressed more than once, is up to them. Each can then make himself as different from the next man as he likes. There is indeed plenty of room for the development of individuality before this point: different parts of the common compulsory curriculum will no doubt pull individuals in different directions, attracting some more towards poetry, others to a life of physical adventure, and so on; and the voluntary system as outlined in chapter 5 will give everyone plenty of further scope for following his own bent.

It is also likely that our present educational system produces less diversity of interests, tastes, etc. than the 'basic minimum' alternative. For as things are the great majority of the population is cut off from the more sophisticated forms of thought and activity. A people whose leisure activities are restricted by their inadequate education to the familiar gamut from drink and sport to TV serials, motor cars and do-it-yourself, are identical in this respect: that this is all they have been equipped to do. We are already too close to the carbon-copy society which right-wing propagandists fear.

In short, fear of uniformity as such is an emotion manufactured by the propagandist. By playing down the need always to qualify talk of uniformity by giving it a context, opponents of a uniform basic education can illicitly associate uniformity in this context with the uniformity of a carbon-copy society and let the revulsion provoked by the latter be transferred to the former. But there is no need to be frightened by words.

Objection 5. 'The last reply persists in missing the point. An intellectually oriented education of the kind described might well be suitable for some, i.e. for those with the innate mental capacity to take it. But it will not do for everybody since not everybody has this capacity. "Ought" implies "can": it is pointless insisting that children should get on the inside of pure mathematics, theoretical physics, philosophy, etc. if they lack the natural ability to do so. This is why uniformity of educational provision will not do. The central objective should be to tailor the curriculum far more closely to what each individual can manage. Those of lower ability tend to be neglected under present arrangements. They tend to be given a "watered down" version of an academic curriculum which only leaves them bored and frustrated. They deserve a new deal: a curriculum perhaps on Newsom, perhaps on other lines, constructed especially for them.'

A particular example of this kind of argument is a recent essay by Professor G. H. Bantock (1971), 'Towards a theory of popular education'. He is especially concerned about the welfare of children of low achievement in 'the bottom stream in small secondary modern schools, in the bottom two or three streams in larger modern and comprehensive schools'. His thesis is that most of these children, if placed in their historico-sociological setting, belong to what he calls the 'folk'. 'In pre-industrial times there were two broad cultures – that based on literacy for the sophisticated and that based on an oral tradition for the folk.' Since universal education began in 1870 it has gone wildly astray in trying to foist a culture based on literacy, intellectual achievement, abstract thinking on children from this folk-group. The question that faces us, Bantock says is: ' "Can we find a syllabus which will be at once demanding but which, based on different principles from the current one will afford greater opportunities to those who at present show little aptitude for the cognitively based curriculum?" I believe it is, and that its basis should be affective-artistic rather than cognitive-intellectual.' Bantock does not favour a Newsomist emphasis on practical activities for these children, so much as an 'education of the emotions'. 'The fundamental discipline of a revised educational system for those who have found the culture of the book almost totally unacceptable is the art of movement with its emphasis on motor skills, communal participation and the opportunity to develop perception and empathy.' From this fundamental discipline children can branch out into dance, music, mime, drama, art and craft, film-making and photography. All this, together with games and physical education, should take up about three-fifths of the children's time, the rest being occupied by preparation for domestic life and technical work 'which would exploit especially the boys' interest in some of the mechanical inventions by which they are surrounded.'

This is Bantock's alternative to the more utilitarian curriculum of the Newsom Report. It has more of a theoretical backing. Anyone who recommends a non-intellectual curriculum for children deemed incapable of it faces the problem of justification. The Newsom Report is especially feeble here. Its main theme is that low ability children need to do woodwork, housecraft, computation, etc. because they will be using such skills in their adult life. This is a pernicious argument, since it prejudges what kind of adult life these children will be leading, thus preventing them from choosing this life for themselves. While there is an echo of this in Bantock's enthusiasm for lessons on domestic life, his main point about an education of the emotions and the centrality in this of aesthetic activities of a physical kind is basically a Platonic one. Like Plato, Bantock holds that there is a division in the human soul between reason and emotion. Emotion is much more obviously a physical phenomenon than reason. Some of us are born with a primarily intellectual orientation, others with a primarily affective one. Education is a matter of developing that part of us which functions best. Rather as Plato's 'children of bronze' are not to be taught mathematics or philosophy but must receive an aesthetic education tied to the world of sense, by which their passionate natures could acquire a kind of harmony, so, too, must Bantock's children of the folk (*Republic*, Plato, Bks 2, 3, 6, 7). Not reason but emotion; not mental skills but physical skills; not abstractions but concrete realities; not the cognitive but the aesthetic; each succeeding dichotomy in Bantock is identified with its predecessor – and each one, together with the identification of each with each, goes straight back to Plato.

But these Platonic dichotomies and identifications are full of logical difficulties. To take just Bantock's main assumption. There in fact, is no division between a rational part of the soul and an emotional one. Emotions imply beliefs and these beliefs can be rationally as well as irrationally based. Fearing X, for instance, implies believing that X is likely to harm one. But fear of poisonous snakes in the jungle is a rational emotion while fear of nonpoisonous spiders is not. Emotions, then, can be rational (see Peters, 1972): this alone knocks the main plank out of the theory. There are other, subsidiary, ones: the assumption that children who pursue more abstract forms of thought are outside the affective domain (one can be as passionately involved with one's calculus as one is with one's clay-modelling); or that aesthetic education must be based on bodily activity (while it is clear from preceding arguments in this essay that it could, and should, be founded rather on contemplation of aesthetic objects, helping one to a fuller understanding of what art is).

Perhaps little more needs to be added about other, largely historical, inadequacies in Bantock's thesis. Leaving aside its curious claim that most low-stream children are descendants of a preindustrial 'folk' (which presumably the rest of us are not), it also makes the charge that a century of trying has failed to get these children inside the more abstract ways of thinking required by an intellectual curriculum. This is simply false. Most of this time has been devoted, at least at a political level, to ensuring that most children never come anywhere near more sophisticated forms of thought. As if the ruling classes had done all they could for a hundred years to equip the children of the masses with new knowledge, new powers, new aspirations which could only undermine their own hegemony!

It is time to leave the idiosyncrasies of Bantock's argument and examine another of his basic assumptions, which will bring us back to the nub of Objection 5. Not all children, it is claimed, have the mental capacity to follow the kind of curriculum I have been advocating. In Bantock's words, 'children differ ineluctably in capacity for both intellectual and affective experience – heredity alone sees to that.' This sort of claim is often made. It has indeed been a basic postulate of educational theory for most of this century. As such it often gets taken for granted as an obvious truth which does not need to be questioned. But where, after all, is the evidence for it?

Perhaps we should ask a prior question. What kind of evidence would be sufficient to show that a child was constitutionally incapable of following an intellectually demanding curriculum? Would a low score on an intelligence test be sufficient? I cannot see that it would. A person may score badly on intelligence tests for a variety of reasons. (i) He may have acquired the necessary skills to do well but fail to apply these skills on a specific occasion owing to, e.g. emotional disturbance or plain lack of interest. (ii) He may lack the concepts necessary to answer the questions set or lack practice at tests of this sort. (iii) He may be constitutionally incapable of scoring more highly. A poor IQ score fails to pinpoint (iii) as the crucial factor. If, as might be the case, it is caused by (i) or (ii), there is no reason to think that the child is incapable of a higher score given therapy or encouragement in the case of (i) and instruction or practice in the case of (ii).

A low IQ cannot therefore be a ground for denying a child a demanding curriculum. Neither, for similar reasons, can poor scholastic performance. If a child is slow to learn, that is not a reason for shunting him in a different direction. If it is important for any child to master the 'basic minimum' curriculum – and I have tried to show that it is supremely important – we have a very good reason, in fact, for spending more time and energy teaching the slower child than we spend on others.

What, then, would be a good ground for the claim in question? If one had some way of telling that a child had reached his intellectual ceiling and that this ceiling was below the level required by the curriculum, that would be adequate. In some cases we do have such a test. We can say pretty safely that such and such a severe mental defective will never go beyond a certain point – say beyond responding to certain simple signs to learning a language as we know it – because however hard his teachers try, whatever different approaches they adopt in getting him to go further, they never succeed. Similarly, we can say with confidence that a child whose vocal chords have been irreparably destroyed will never show intelligence as a parliamentary debater. Here it is his physical state rather than trial and error that makes it clear that however hard we try we shall never be successful. It is true that even in these cases we cannot know this for certain: brain-transfers or artificial vocal chords may come to be and prove us wrong. But, even so, barring these, we have good grounds for claiming that there are ceilings here: namely, the failure of the most strenuous efforts to get beyond a certain point, or an obvious physical incapacity which makes such efforts superfluous.

But we may not have these good grounds where normal children are concerned. If, for instance, a child finds a new part of mathematics insuperably difficult, what shall we say? That he will not ever be able to master it, that it just is not in him? Or that we have not found the right method of getting him to learn? There is a good reason to prefer the latter alternative. This is the nature of the gap between what the child can do and what he cannot. The child already knows a little mathematics. He has mastered stage X in the syllabus; but he cannot reach stage Y. He is in a very different position from the severe mental defective. For the latter's stumbling-block is language itself: it is not an inability to extend an already established conceptual scheme, but rather an inability to grasp any concepts, or, in the less severe cases, to grasp any in a more than superficial way. That some people should be unable ever to leap this immense chasm is readily intelligible, given some explanation in terms of brain-damage, etc., but that someone should fail irredeemably to cotton on to algebra with a good basis in arithmetic, or to learn long division with a good basis in simple division is all but incredible. What idiots can bring to their learning is limited:

this limits the methods employable: so there comes a time when their teachers can say, 'We have tried every method available, but failed.' But once a child has learned a language, he has in his possession a store of tools – the concepts which he can grasp – which not only he can use but which his teachers can, too, to help him over the next step. Both if his inability is intellectual, or if it is more a matter of lack of interest, there are innumerable ways in which these tools can be fitted together to make this or that appeal. For this reason, even if a teacher fails to get the child to learn, he can never be so sure as the idiot's teacher that all available methods have failed.

Let us apply this criterion to the claim that children differ ineluctably in mental capacity. If one accepts the evidence that some extreme mental defectives do have unalterable ceilings, which normal children surpass, then the claim is validated to that extent. But this is hardly relevant to the controversy aroused by Objection 5, since this claims that there are individual differences in innate mental capacity among normal children. This claim may be true. Some self-styled environmentalists go too far in asserting that environmental improvements can bring all children up to the same intellectual level, i.e. that there are no insuperable barriers blocking some children's progress. This is pure dogma. But so is the innatist claim with which it is often contrasted. To repeat: it may be true that there are individual differences in innate mental capacity among normals: but this is something which is probably not empirically verifiable and is certainly not empirically falsifiable. It is probably not verifiable given the difficulty, mentioned above, of proving that any normal person who gets intellectually stuck and fails to respond to all kinds of attempts to shift him has indeed reached his constitutional ceiling. It is certainly not falsifiable since one could never show that someone had no ceiling: even the most clever man in the world might have his Pons Asinorum somewhere. It gives every appearance, therefore, of being an example of the untestable kind of axiom one often finds presupposed to ideological systems, of being to the ideology that has accreted around the intelligence test what the equally untestable proposition that Christ is the son of God is to Christianity or what the thesis of economic determinism is to Marxism.

Bantock's whole thesis, as he admits in his essay, rests on this belief in ineluctable differences in mental capacity. But it is not a rational belief. It is, rather, an article of faith. The same is true of many other writers of his persuasion: unquestioned and unquestionable, this proposition has been the linch-pin of the most powerful ideology of our seemingly so unideological society.

99

There is a further point. Even if one accepts the dogma as an article of faith, it still does not follow that individual differences in capacity are such that they prevent some children from being able to follow a sophisticated curriculum. For it is even consistent with this dogma that all normal children could, say, get a first degree: their individually different ceilings might only operate above this point. So Bantock's untestable belief in 'ineluctable differences' is still not enough to justify his folk-curriculum. He would have at least to show that teachers had made all sorts of attempts to teach his low ability children things like mathematics, physics and so on, and that every such attempt had failed. This would be a start, if not conclusive. But he cannot of course show this, because it has not happened. His unsupported gesturings to a hundred years of futile efforts on their behalf do nothing for his case.

Objection 6. 'Part of Objection 5 still stands. There cannot be a uniformly academic curriculum for everyone. It is all very well for people not teaching in schools to put forward this kind of ideal. In principle it is fine. But we live in a real world, not in Utopia. Perhaps the boys and girls in class IV D of the average secondary modern school are, in fact, innately capable of learning the binomial theorem. But one will not get very far in practice if one tries to teach it to them. An academic curriculum is not for them. It may be difficult to say what is, but some alternative must be found. It is this kind of consideration which lay behind the Newsom Report's recommendations for the thirteen- to sixteen-year-old low-ability children with whom it was concerned.'

This is another Janus argument, which can be taken in more than one way. If it is interpreted as referring to children now (in 1973) in their last year or so of school, it is doubtless true to a large extent. It is hardly likely that pupils of fourteen or fifteen, who know virtually nothing of art, science, or mathematics and whose interests pull them away from school to other things, would be able to reach the basic minimum by the time they left school in a year or eighteen months. There is indeed a serious problem of knowing what kind of curriculum is best suited for them.

But interpreted this way, this is no real objection to the main thesis, for this is concerned not with children leaving school in 1973 but with children who are being born in 1973 (and later). If they follow a rationally worked out curriculum there is some hope that none of them will reach their teens ignorant and alienated from school. There is no reason to think that the problem of what to do with the IV D toughs need remain with us for ever.

But there is more to be said about Objection 6. Interpreted one way, it presents no challenge to the main thesis. It deals with a possibly short-term emergency: the thesis lays down long-term plans. But it is not always clear that those who adopt Objection 6 are thinking only in the short term. The work of the Schools Council is a curious example of this. The Schools Council was set up in 1964, soon after the Newsom Report was published in 1963. A large part of its remit, adumbrated in its constitution and crystallized at its inaugural meetings, has been to follow through the implications of the Newsom Report and set up a series of projects on curricula for the 'Young School Leaver', i.e. for the pupil who leaves school at the minimum age of sixteen. Now that it has published many working papers on these projects it should be possible to see in broad terms what kind of recommendations for the young school leaver it is making. Unfortunately, no clear picture emerges. This is largely because the criteria for identifying the 'young school leaver' are left obscure. If one looks at the Council's work on the humanities side, it looks as if he is to be identified as the pupil of thirteen or fourteen who has little interest in school and wants to leave. But the Foreword to Working Paper no. 14 on 'Mathematics for the Majority' tells us that the current YSL projects are to be the bases of 'relevant and useful five-year courses for pupils leaving school at sixteen'. The young school leaver is thus identifiable, not in his last year or so at school, but as early as eleven: for it is then that he will have to begin his five-year course. If this is so, then the YSL schemes are not concerned with emergency curricula for the 'IV D toughs', but rather with curricula covering the whole five years of secondary education. One cannot but conclude from the above short quotation that the Schools Council is recommending one kind of five-year course for those who will leave at sixteen and another for those staying on. But on what basis is a child to be identified at eleven as someone who will be leaving at sixteen? How can one tell this five years before it happens? There is no need for us to go back through earlier arguments about innate mental capacities. There is just no valid way of making such predictions. If it is indeed recommending a forking of the roads at eleven, the Schools Council leaves us precisely where we were under the selective system we have known since 1902. If, on the other hand, what it wants is not a five-year course at eleven for those who will leave at sixteen but a common course for those who may or may not be leaving at sixteen, that is an entirely different suggestion and one quite in line with this essay's thesis. It is not at all clear which of these alternatives the Council has in mind.

There is one further point to be made about YSL schemes in the first sense of the term, i.e. about emergency final year courses. There is nothing wrong with these in principle if they are only very short-term expedients. But short-term expedients often have a habit of growing into permanent institutions and if this happened with the YSL schemes, this might set back the educational advancement of the ordinary child for decades; these schemes take the present kind of education for those at present leaving at fifteen entirely as given. Given what we now have, they ask what can teachers do, once the school leaving age is raised to sixteen, with a pupil 'in his extra year'? It is not surprising that the general verdict of the various YSL projects so far worked out in different fields would seem to be: not very much. The Humanities Project, for instance, may enable him to express his own views and hear those of his classmates on war and violence and poverty; but without a thorough grounding in relevant information, in all the problems of fact and value which surround these immense issues, it is hard to see that very much can be achieved; it is like building a roof with no house to go beneath it. It cannot be a long-term solution to work out last-year projects in this way. As short-term expedients for children immediately faced with an extra year's schooling they may be better than nothing. But how short is short? The Schools Council set in motion its first research on YSL curricula in 1964. It was then a matter of some urgency. It is still continuing. This adds up already to nearly ten years spent in developing emergency curricula – years which could and should have been devoted to a more radical reconstruction. It is as if a Ministry of Housing, alarmed by a temporary crisis, spent a whole decade designing a cheap dwelling made of cardboard while thousands went in need of decent flats and houses. The danger is, in education as in housing, that temporary structures have a habit of becoming permanent. The emergency final-year projects might, if we are not careful, become the crown of the slower child's school career: work lower down the school might be planned to lead up to them. In the interests of the next generation we must see that this does not happen. We have wasted too many years already designing various devices to fix the end-points of children's school careers as maxima beyond which they cannot go. We could do worse than begin our second century of universal education by avoiding any more of the successive waves of reformist or progressivist enthusiasm which for seventy years have washed us back on to this same bit of shingle – E. G. A. Holmes's ideology of 'natural growth' in the 1900s; the emergence of the intelligence test in the 1910s and 1920s as the new saviour of the bright working-class child; the call for 'practical' education under Hadow in the 1920s, echoed by Newsom in the 1960s; and the contemporary vogue for cafeteria curricula, the elimination of subject-mindedness, E. and V. counselling and special courses for the young school leaver. We could even be revolutionary enough to put ourselves back in the position of the pioneers of 1870 and begin by seeing how far we can agree together on some basic minima.

Notes

Chapter 2

1 Part of chapter VI of *Ethics and Education* continues the discussion of intrinsically worth-while activities found in chapter V. The claim is here that practical activities, e.g. politics and cookery, may be no less worth while than theoretical pursuits. But it appears that, in so far as we are concerned with their intrinsic worth (the extrinsic justification of them is obvious), they, too, are said to be worth while in a way that games and pastimes are not, provided they have a theoretical under-pinning. 'Because they are partly dependent, in respect of their quality, on the level of understanding that goes into them, their degree of worth-whileness must depend in part on the pursuit of truth in its different forms which they sustain and by which they are transformed' (p. 176). It is because practical activities are in this way held to be parasitic on the theoretical activities of chapter V that I concentrate on the latter.

2 I owe the line of thought in this paragraph to Mr R. K. Elliott.

Chapter 3

1 I am using 'activities' to cover not only activities in the usual sense, but also passive enjoyments like being tickled or getting sunburnt.

2 'Speech' here includes the use of deaf-and-dumb language. Linguistic communication is being considered in this chapter as an end in itself. Its instrumental side will be touched on below in chapter 4.

3 I am grateful to Keith Thompson for his criticisms at this point.

4 'Compelled' here should not be read as 'coerced'. What I mean is that it cannot be left to the child to say whether or not he will learn mathe-matics, for instance: the fundamental curricular principles which I have described would not be attainable if he left school without knowing any. This does not imply that the child must be dragooned to study anything. Other methods are surely possible, both more humane and probably more efficient. It is easy to overlook this distinction between 'compulsion' and 'coercion'. P. S. Wilson, for instance, in his *Interest and Discipline in Education* (1971) misunderstands an earlier essay of mine in favour of a compulsory curriculum ('Learn as you will', *New Society*, 4 December 1969). He wrongly asserts that when I write that children must be made to study certain academic disciplines, this implies that I favour the application of psychological and perhaps even physical pressures to force

them to do so. It should be clear from the emphasis I place on the child's liberty in this present work that nothing could be further from the truth.

Chapter 4

1 E.g. Schools Council Working Paper no. 11. This criticism cannot be made of the later *Schools Council Integrated Studies* (O.U.P., 1972). On 'Sociological English', see also E. Shayer, *The Teaching of English in Schools, 1900–1970* (Routledge & Kegan Paul, 1972), pp. 171-9.

Chapter 5

1 It is a weakness of our specialized system of higher education in the arts that we produce, in fact, very few such people with a wide knowledge of the arts as a whole.

2 See N. Grant, *Society, Schools and Progress in Eastern Europe* (Pergamon, 1969), pp. 123-33. My points about voluntary education draw heavily on my 'Learn as you will', *New Society*, 4 December 1969.

Chapter 6

1 The use of 'physicalistic' would still raise problems, since concepts like 'hot water bottle', 'watch' or 'telephone' are only intelligible in terms of what people want to use these things for, thus introducing 'mentalistic' concepts. Concepts of this sort, which Dearden usefully calls 'practical' concepts as distinct from 'perceptual' concepts like 'red' and 'smooth' (1968, ch. 6), straddle the mental-physical divide. This makes it all the more difficult to parcel out our concepts into the area mentioned in the areas: 'practical' concepts would be neither just mentalistic nor just physicalistic, but both. Dearden's threefold – avowedly not exhaustive – division of concepts into 'practical', 'perceptual' and 'theoretical' avoids this particular difficulty, since the concepts found in the 'forms of understanding' are only the 'theoretical' ones.

Chapter 7

1 I am using 'beauty' to stand for aesthetic values in general.

2 The 'E. and V.' counsellor helps pupils to choose curriculum courses and to choose careers. The first is the 'educational', the second the 'vocational' side of his work. Both sides, of course, are closely related. For a fuller discussion of counselling, from which much of the material here is drawn, see my 'The concept of the school counsellor,' in *Education for Teaching*, summer 1970.

Bibliography

ADAMS, M. (1969), 'Reply to R. Carlisle', *Proceedings of the Philosophy of Education Society of Great Britain*, vol. III, January 1969.

BANTOCK, G. H. (1971), 'Towards a theory of popular education', in Hooper, R. (ed.), *The Curriculum: Context, Design and Development*, Oliver & Boyd.

BRUNER, J. S. (1960), *The Process of Education*, Vintage Books, New York.

BURCKHARDT, J. (1860), *The Civilisation of the Renaissance in Italy*, Mentor Books, New York, 1961.

CARLISLE, R. (1969), 'The concept of physical education', *Proceedings of the Philosophy of Education Society of Great Britain*, vol. III, January 1969.

DEARDEN, R. F. (1968), *The Philosophy of Primary Education*, Routledge & Kegan Paul.

FINDLAY, J. N. (1970). *Axiological Ethics*, Macmillan.

GALLIE, W. B. (1964), *Philosophy and the Historical Understanding*, Chatto & Windus.

GRANT, N. (1969), *Schools, Society and Progress in Eastern Europe*, Pergamon.

HIRST, P. H. (1965), 'Liberal education and the nature of knowledge', in Archambault, R. D. (ed.), *Philosophical Analysis and Education*, Routledge & Kegan Paul.

HIRST, P. H. and PETERS, R. S. (1970), *The Logic of Education*, Routledge & Kegan Paul.

HORNSEY, A. W. (1969), 'Why teach a foreign language?' *University of London Institute of Education Bulletin*, no. 18, summer 1969.

KIERKEGAARD, S. K. (1843), *Either/Or*, Anchor Books, New York, 1959.

MACINTYRE, A. C. (1958), *The Unconscious*, Routledge & Kegan Paul.

MARTIN, J. R. (1970), 'The disciplines and the curriculum', in her collection, *Readings in the Philosophy of Education: A Study of Curriculum*, Allyn & Bacon, Boston.

MILL, JAMES (1825), 'On education', *Encyclopaedia Britannica*.

MILL, JOHN STUART (1863), *Utilitarianism* (many editions).

MOORE, G. E. (1903), *Principia Ethica*, Cambridge University Press.

NEWSOM REPORT (1963), *Half our Future*, HMSO.

NEWTON, A. W. (1919), *The English Elementary School*, Longmans.

PETERS, R. S. (1966), *Ethics and Education*, Allen & Unwin.

PETERS, R. S. (1972), 'The education of the emotions' in Dearden, R. F., Hirst, P. H. and Peters, R. S. (eds), *Education and the Development of Reason*, Routledge & Kegan Paul.

PETERS, R. S. (see also HIRST, P. H. and PETERS, R. S.).

PHENIX, P. H. (1964), *Realms of Meaning*, McGraw-Hill, New York.

PLATO, *Republic* (many editions).

SCHEFFLER, I. (1970), 'Justifying curriculum decisions', in Martin, J. R. (ed.), *Readings in Philosophy of Education: A Study of Curriculum*, Allyn & Bacon, Boston.

VAUGHAN, T. D. (1970), *Education and Vocational Guidance Today*, Routledge & Kegan Paul.

WHITE, J. P. (1968), 'Creativity and education', *British Journal of Educational Studies*, vol. XVI, no. 2, June 1968.

WHITE, P. A. (1971), 'Education, democracy and the public interest', *Proceedings of the Philosophy of Education Society of Great Britain*, vol. V, no. 1, 1971.

WILSON, P. S. (1971), *Interest and Discipline in Education*, Routledge & Kegan Paul.

WRIGHT, G. H. VON (1963), *The Varieties of Goodness*, Routledge & Kegan Paul.

Suggestions for further reading

Two recent American books on the structure of the curriculum as a whole are Broudy, H. S., Smith, B. O. and Burnett, J. R., *Democracy and Excellence in the American Secondary School* (Rand-McNally, 1964) and Phenix, P. H., *Realms of Meaning* (McGraw-Hill, 1964). Each of these has its own distinctive categorization of preferred curriculum objectives. So, too, does a book which I only came across having completed this essay: J. F. Herbart's *The Science of Education*, 1806; translated by H. M. and E. Felkin (Swan Sonnenschein, London, 1892). This is now a little-known work, although at the turn of the century a fairly influential one in this country. Not easy to read, but worth persevering with, it remains a well-articulated, broadly philosophical account of, among other things, the aims of education and their realization in a course of study. Herbart is especially interesting for his emphasis on the 'integrative' side of education, which I briefly discussed in chapter 4, and for his discussion of the importance of developing a 'many-sided interest' to satisfy the claims both of individual fulfilment and of morality. Morality is for Herbart the supreme aim of education: I found his discussion of this a necessary corrective to the individualistic point of view I adopted in most of this book. A useful account of Herbart's curiously short-lived popularity in English educational circles between about 1890 and 1914 is to be found in Selleck, R. J. W., *The New Education: The English Background, 1870-1914* (Pitman, 1968). This book also discusses other prominent educational theories of the time, e.g. those advocating practical studies and the extreme 'child-centred' ideology of E. G. A. Holmes. I found it invaluable for seeing our contemporary clash of curriculum theories and practices in its historical perspective.

Turning to articles or chapters (rather than whole books) on curriculum activities and their justification, a useful collection is Martin, J. R., *Readings in the Philosophy of Education: A Study of*

Curriculum (Allyn & Bacon, Boston, 1970). It should also go with-out saying, from my detailed discussion of them in the text, that one should look at Peters, R. S., *Ethics and Education* (Allen & Unwin, 1966) chapters 5 and 6, and Hirst, P. H., 'Liberal education and the nature of knowledge' in Archambault, R. D. (ed.), *Philosophical Analysis and Education* (Routledge & Kegan Paul, 1965). There are now a number of elaborations and critical discussions of these two seminal studies, some of which have only come to my notice since completing the book. The critical discussions are of varying quality. I include all those which to my knowledge have been published to date (January 1973) as a guide to those who want a survey of the literature available.

On Peters's theory of worth-while activities Peters himself pro-vides a further elucidation in 'The justification of education' in Peters, R. S. (ed.), *Oxford Readings in Philosophy: Philosophy of Education* (O.U.P., 1973). There are discussions of the theory in Wilson, P. S., 'In defence of bingo' in *British Journal of Educational Studies*, June 1967 (with a rejoinder by Peters in the same issue); Powell, J. P., 'On justifying a broad educational curriculum' in *Educational Philosophy and Theory* (*EPT*), March 1970; and Robin-son, K., 'Education and initiation', *EPT*, October 1970.

On Hirst's theory of forms of knowledge, elaborations are to be found in Dearden, R. F., *The Philosophy of Primary Education* (Routledge & Kegan Paul, 1968) chapter 4; Hirst, P. H., 'Educational theory' in Tibble J. W. (ed.), *The Study of Education* (Routledge & Kegan Paul, 1966), chapter 2; Hirst, P. H. and Peters, R. S., *The Logic of Education* (Routledge & Kegan Paul, 1970), chapter 4. There are discussions of the theory in general in Martin, J. R., 'The disciplines and the curriculum', *EPT*, 1969 (included in Martin, J. R., 1970); Phillips, D. C., 'The distinguishing features of forms of knowledge', *EPT*, October 1971; and Hindess, E., 'Forms of knowledge', *Proceedings of the Philosophy of Education Society of Great Britain* (*PPES*), supplementary issue, vol. VI, no. 2, 1972. Papers on the arts as a form of knowledge are Gribble, J., 'Forms of knowledge', *EPT*, March 1970; Hirst's reply, 'Literature, criticism and the forms of knowledge', *EPT*, April 1971; and an interesting paper by Greger, S., 'Aesthetic meaning' in *PPES*, supplementary issue, vol. VI, no. 2, 1972.

A tantalizingly short paragraph in Winch, R., *The Idea of a Social Science* (Routledge & Kegan Paul, 1958), p. 109, gives me some comfort that my distinction between category I and category II activities is not an idiosyncratic aberration of my own.

Index